SMP interact

9T

Book 9T

D0524925

CAMBRIDGE
UNIVERSITY PRESS

PUBLISHED BY THE PRESS SYNDICATE OF THE UNIVERSITY OF CAMBRIDGE
The Pitt Building, Trumpington Street, Cambridge, United Kingdom

CAMBRIDGE UNIVERSITY PRESS
The Edinburgh Building, Cambridge CB2 2RU, UK
40 West 20th Street, New York, NY 10011-4211, USA
477 Williamstown Road, Port Melbourne, VIC 3207, Australia
Ruiz de Alarcón 13, 28014 Madrid, Spain
Dock House, The Waterfront, Cape Town 8001, South Africa

http://www.cambridge.org/

Printed in the United Kingdom at the University Press, Cambridge

Typeface Minion   *System* QuarkXPress®

A catalogue record for this book is available from the British Library

ISBN 0 521 53819 X paperback

Typesetting and technical illustrations by The School Mathematics Project
Other illustrations by Robert Calow and Steve Lach at Eikon Illustration
Cover image © ImageState Ltd
Cover design by Angela Ashton

The publishers thank the following for supplying photographs:
Page 106 © Simon Fraser/Science Photo Library
Page 108 Geranium © Mark Bolton/Garden Image/Oxford Scientific Films
          Sweet pea © Flowerphotos/Carol Sharp
Pages 109 and 110 Paul Scruton
Pages 121, 133 and 138 Graham Portlock
Page 130 © Colin Baxter

We have been unable to trace the copyright holder of the photograph on page 19 (from Robin
Fabish, *New Zealand Maori: Culture and Craft* (Auckland: Hodder Moa Beckett, 1995), p. 40) and
would be grateful for any information that would enable us to do so.

The authors and publishers would like to thank Evan Sedgwick-Jell for his help with the
production of this book.

NOTICE TO TEACHERS
It is illegal to reproduce any part of this work in material form (including photocopying and
electronic storage) except under the following circumstances:
(i) when you are abiding by a licence granted to your school or institution by the Copyright
Licensing Agency;
(ii) where no such licence exists, or where you wish to exceed the terms of a licence, and you have
gained the written permission of Cambridge University Press;
(iii) where you are allowed to reproduce without permission under the provisions of Chapter 3
of the Copyright, Designs and Patents Act 1988.

Contents

1 Number bites *4*

2 Clock polygons *10*

3 Decimals *11*

4 Making rules *19*

5 Fractions *29*

Review 1 *36*

6 Probability *38*

7 Earning money *45*

8 Garden centre *47*

9 Percentages *48*

10 Square deal *54*

11 Pie charts *62*

12 Probability experiments *67*

Review 2 *73*

13 Division *75*

14 Bottles *83*

15 Transformations *84*

16 Groundwork *91*

17 Number relationships *94*

18 Simplifying *99*

19 Two-way tables *106*

Review 3 *111*

20 Angles and lines *113*

21 True or false? *123*

22 Time and timetables *124*

23 More negative numbers *130*

24 Ratio *136*

Review 4 *141*

Index *143*

① Number bites

These are short activities to give you regular practice of your number skills.
You don't need to do them all in one bite. Just use each one when you need it.

W Whole numbers

W1 Two-digit numbers

In these questions, each digit may be used only once.

1 Use these digits to make three 2-digit numbers.
   • The first must be a multiple of 3.
   • The second must be a multiple of 5.
   • The third must be a multiple of 7.

| 1 | 2 | 3 | 4 | 5 | 6 |

For example, this is a multiple of 3.

| 2 | 4 |

2 Use these digits to make three 2-digit numbers.
   • The first must be a multiple of 7.
   • The second must be a multiple of 8.
   • The third must be a multiple of 9.

| 2 | 3 | 4 | 5 | 6 | 7 |

3 Use as many of these digits as you can to make a set of 2-digit numbers
   which are all multiples of 8.

| 0 | 1 | 2 | 3 | 4 | 5 | 6 | 7 | 8 | 9 |

W2 Chairs

A school caretaker has to lay out chairs for a school concert.
He is asked to put out 25 rows of 18 chairs. He has 420 chairs.

Does he have enough chairs?

Will he have enough chairs for

(a)	32 rows of 12	(b)	27 rows of 16	(c)	21 rows of 20
(d)	21 rows of 21	(e)	28 rows of 15	(f)	38 rows of 11

W3 Leave it out!

Make up a calculation whose answer is 135, but does not use the digits 1, 3 or 5.
You may use the other digits more than once.

Do the same for

(a)	247	(b)	201	(c)	169	(d)	420	(c)	348

W4 Clues

Use the clues to find the numbers.

1
- It is smaller than 500.
- All the digits are the same.
- It has 3 as a factor.
- It has 4 as a factor.

2
- It is smaller than 20.
- When you divide it by 2, the remainder is 1.
- When you divide it by 3, the remainder is 2.
- When you divide it by 4, the remainder is 3.

3
- It is an odd number.
- It is greater than 100.
- It is smaller than 200.
- Add its digits and you get 15.
- Two digits are the same.

4
- It is a three-digit number.
- One of its factors is 5.
- The total of its digits is 10.
- The digits multiply to give 30.
- The hundreds digit is less than the tens digit.
- The tens digit is less than the units digit.

5
- It is a three-digit number.
- It is a multiple of 5.
- Multiply the tens digits and the units digit and you get 30.
- Multiply the hundreds digit and the units digit and you get 5.
- The total of all the digits is 12.

W5 Sporty words

Work out each answer.
Use the code to find a word connected with sport.

0	1	2	3	4	5	6	7	8	9
L	O	T	A	G	D	S	P	F	R

Example: $118 \times 35 = $ **4 1 3 0**

G O A L

| 1 | 89×8 | 2 | 821×5 | 3 | 89×33 | 4 | 79×52 |
| 5 | 364×25 | 6 | 263×27 | 7 | 709×88 | 8 | 914×59 |

W6 Cover up

You need sheet 266.

Cut out the eight pieces and put them on the board. Each piece can go this way

or this way

multiples of 3	multiples of 4
square numbers	factors of 20
odd numbers	even numbers
factors of 24	prime numbers

15	12	11	19
9	16	25	5
6	8	49	1
2	5	4	10

F Fractions

F1 What fraction?

What fraction of each of these shapes is shaded?

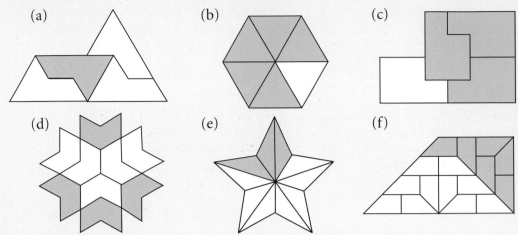

(a) (b) (c)

(d) (e) (f)

Draw some designs of your own to show some different fractions.

F2 Fractions of words

The first $\frac{1}{3}$ of ACTORS is AC. The last $\frac{3}{5}$ of FLUTE is UTE.
Put them together and you get ACUTE.

What mathematical words do these make?

1 The first $\frac{1}{2}$ of PRISON and the last $\frac{1}{3}$ of SESAME.

2 The first $\frac{1}{3}$ of KILLER and the last $\frac{1}{4}$ of ACCURATE.

3 The first $\frac{3}{4}$ of FACE and the last $\frac{3}{5}$ of MOTOR.

4 The first $\frac{1}{2}$ of FRANCE, the last $\frac{1}{2}$ of DUCT and the last $\frac{3}{4}$ of LION.

5 The first $\frac{1}{3}$ of POLICE, the last $\frac{2}{5}$ of EARLY and the first $\frac{3}{4}$ of GONE.

F3 A fraction of time

1 How many minutes are there in

(a) $\frac{1}{4}$ of an hour (b) $\frac{1}{2}$ of an hour (c) $\frac{1}{10}$ of an hour (d) $\frac{1}{6}$ of an hour

(e) $\frac{3}{4}$ of an hour (f) $\frac{7}{10}$ of an hour (g) $\frac{2}{3}$ of an hour (h) $\frac{5}{12}$ of an hour

2 Write each of these as a fraction of an hour, as simply as possible.

(a) 20 minutes (b) 12 minutes (c) 5 minutes (d) 35 minutes

D Decimals

D1 Number patterns

1 The numbers below this number line go up by 0.6 each time.

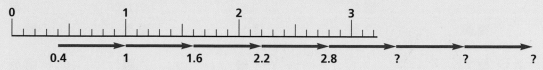

0.4   1   1.6   2.2   2.8   ?   ?   ?

What are the next three numbers after 2.8?

2 The numbers in this pattern go up by 0.3 each time.   2 2.3 2.6 2.9 ... ...
What are the next three numbers in the pattern?

3 Write the next two numbers in each of these patterns.

  (a) 1.3   1.5   1.7   1.9 ... ...   (b) 2.1   2.4   2.7   3 ... ...

  (c) 8.3   8.7   9.1   9.5 ... ...   (d) 6   6.2   6.4   6.6 ... ...

  (e) 8.7   8.5   8.3   8.1 ... ...   (f) 7   6.6   6.2   5.8 ... ...

D2 Bottles

1 Calculate the total amount in each group of bottles.

  (a)   (b)   (c)

 0.4 litre each

 1.5 litres each

 2.4 litres each

2 Calculate the total amount in each of these.

  (a) 8 bottles, each holding 4.7 litres   (b) 4 bottles, each holding 12.8 litres

  (c) 9 bottles, each holding 1.8 litres   (d) 6 bottles, each holding 0.9 litre

D3 Telephone pole

T

Follow the instructions on sheet 267 for this activity.

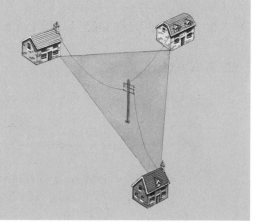

D4 Missing digits

Copy these and fill in the missing digits.

1	2	3	4	5
2.8 + 4.3 ■.■	1.6 + ■.5 3.■	4.■ + 3.8 ■.1	9.3 − 2.7 ■.■	8.4 − 1.■ ■.1

6	7	8	9	10
■.7 − 2.■ 1.3	7.3 − 2.■ ■.5	7.■ − ■.5 2.9	9.■ − ■.5 8.6	■.■ − 2.4 5.6

D5 What's missing?

Copy and complete these.
The missing bit could be a number or × or ÷.

1 $10 \times 6.3 = $ ■

2 $3.1 \times $ ■ $ = 310$

3 420 ■ $10 = 42$

4 0.89 ■ $10 = 8.9$

5 $6.07 \times $ ■ $ = 607$

6 $0.03 \times $ ■ $ = 3$

7 4 ■ ■ $ = 0.04$

8 0.86 ■ ■ $ = 86$

9 ■ $ \div 100 = 0.402$

D6 Made to measure

1 What lengths do the arrows point to?
   Write each length in metres.

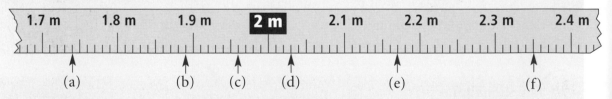

2 Here are the heights and weights of eight people.
   (a) Write the names in order of height, smallest first.
   (b) Write the names in order of weight, lightest first.

Alan	**Becky**	**Carl**	**Dean**
Height 1.74 m Weight 74.65 kg	Height 1.66 m Weight 65.2 kg	Height 1.8 m Weight 84.12 kg	Height 1.42 m Weight 50.7 kg

Erik	**Farnaz**	**Gill**	**Hitesh**
Height 2.02 m Weight 80.71 kg	Height 1.6 m Weight 59 kg	Height 1.09 m Weight 35.82 kg	Height 1.57 m Weight 65.26 kg

D7 Halfway numbers

In each question, make the halfway number using the digits shown here and the decimal point.

| 0 | 1 | 2 | 3 | 5 | 9 | . |

For example, the number which is halfway between 0.8 and 1 is | 0 | . | 9 |

Make the number which is halfway between

1	0.1 and 0.3	**2**	0.1 and 0.5	**3**	0 and 0.5	**4**	0.1 and 0.2
5	0.9 and 1	**6**	0.1 and 0.9	**7**	3 and 4	**8**	1.1 and 1.5
9	0.9 and 1.5	**10**	1 and 1.5	**11**	3.1 and 3.2	**12**	3 and 3.1
13	12 and 13	**14**	9 and 9.1	**15**	0 and 0.7	**16**	12 and 12.1

M A mixed bag

M1 Last orders

These sets of cards have been mixed up and some of the numbers are missing.

Write the numbers in order so that they go up in equal steps each time.
Fill in the missing numbers.

1 20 | ? | 14 | 23 | ? | 29 | 17 | 35

2 60 | ? | 32 | 53 | ? | 25 | 18

3 0.4 | ? | 1.9 | 0.1 | ? | 1.3 | 0.7

4 2 | ? | ⁻4 | 5 | ? | 8 | ⁻10

M2 Day and night (oral)

Place	Noon temperature	Midnight temperature
Sitting room	18°C	7°C
Kitchen	21°C	6°C
Bathroom	14°C	3°C
Attic	11°C	⁻2°C
Garden	9°C	⁻6°C
Garage	10°C	⁻4°C

T

② Clock polygons

This work will help you

- ◆ revise the names of shapes
- ◆ understand the idea of congruence

T

Shapes can be made by joining up the points on a clockface.

Triangles

This scalene triangle has been made by joining 5 to 9 to 12 and back to 5. This can be written 5, 9, 12.

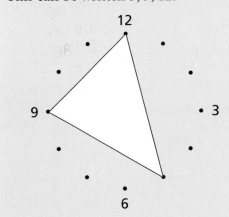

Here is a 2, 7, 10 triangle.

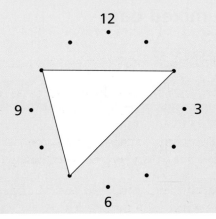

- • Check that the sides and angles of the 2, 7, 10 triangle are the same as the 5, 9, 12 triangle. Triangle 2, 7, 10 is **congruent** to triangle 5, 9, 12. Triangles 2, 7, 10 and 5, 9, 12 are **congruent triangles.**

- • Are there other triangles which are congruent to the 2, 7, 10 and 5, 9, 12 triangles? Find some other sets of congruent triangles.

- • What special types of triangle are these?

  (a) 4, 8, 12   (b) 2, 6, 10   (c) 2, 7, 9   (d) 1, 3, 7

Quadrilaterals

- • What shape is made by joining the numbers 1, 4, 7, 10? What other numbers can be joined to make the same shape?

- • What shape is made by joining the numbers

  (a) 2, 4, 6, 10   (b) 1, 3, 7, 9   (c) 1, 4, 8, 11

- • What other quadrilaterals can be made by joining four points on the clockface?

③ Decimals

This work will help you

- ◆ solve problems with decimals and money
- ◆ round to the nearest penny

A Food for friends

- Gina buys two Napoletana pizzas.
- Mehmet and Molly share the cost of a Margherita pizza.

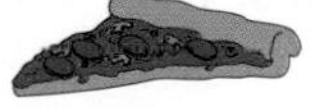

Pizza House

MARGHERITA	£3.60
NAPOLETANA	£4.25
MUSHROOM	£4.20
SICILIANA	£6.05
AMERICAN	£5.80

Do not use a calculator for these questions.

A1 How much will it cost for four Siciliana pizzas?

A2 Two friends share the cost of an American pizza. How much do they each pay?

A3 Simon buys four Margherita pizzas. How much do his pizzas cost altogether?

A4 Three friends share the cost of a Mushroom pizza. How much do they each pay?

A5 Four friends share the cost of a Mushroom and a Margherita pizza. How much do they each pay?

Four friends have a meal at Pizza House.
Their bill is shown below.

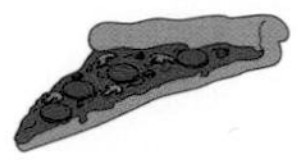

Pizza House

Pizzas	£21.60
Salads	£2.65
	£2.10
6 glasses wine	£11.70
3 coffees	£2.55
Total	**£40.60**

A6 What is the cost of a coffee?

A7 The friends drank six glasses of wine altogether. How much does one glass of wine cost?

A8 The four friends decide to share the cost of the meal equally. How much do they each pay for the meal?

B Shopping

Mushrooms	Onions	Tomatoes	New Potatoes	Peppers
£2.40 per kg	£0.52 per kg	£1.40 per kg	£0.26 per kg	£2.84 per kg

Do not use a calculator for questions B1 and B2.

B1 Work out the cost of

(a) 2 kg of mushrooms

(b) 3 kg of new potatoes

(c) 5 kg of tomatoes

(d) 2 kg of peppers

(e) 4 kg of mushrooms

(f) 6 kg of new potatoes

(g) 3 kg of peppers

(h) $\frac{1}{2}$ kg of tomatoes

(i) $\frac{1}{2}$ kg of onions

(j) $1\frac{1}{2}$ kg of peppers

B2 In these packs, what is the cost of

(a) a pot of yoghurt

(b) a chocolate biscuit

(c) a fruit drink

4 yoghurts
£1.20

Six fruit drinks
£2.10

Five biscuits
£1.55

You may use a calculator for questions B3 and B4.

B3 What is the cost of

(a) 1.6 kg of mushrooms

(b) 3.5 kg of new potatoes

(c) 5.7 kg of tomatoes

(d) 2.5 kg of peppers

(e) 3.9 kg of mushrooms

(f) 6.5 kg of new potatoes

(g) 0.5 kg of peppers

(h) 0.3 kg of tomatoes

B4 A pack of 24 bags of crisps cost £3.12.
What is the cost of a bag of crisps in this pack?

C Rounding

A garden centre sells wild bird food from tubs.

3.2 kg of sunflower seed costs

3.2 × £1.68 = £5.376

   = £5.38 (to the nearest penny)

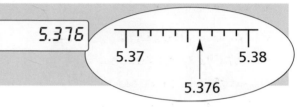

5.376

5.37   5.376   5.38

Use a calculator to answer these questions.

C1 To the nearest penny, work out the cost of

(a) 1.2 kg of peanuts

(b) 3.6 kg of wild bird seed

(c) 2.7 kg of sunflower seed

(d) 4.8 kg of premium bird seed

(e) 3.5 kg of wild bird seed

(f) 0.8 kg of sunflower seed

(g) 1.5 kg of sunflower seed

(h) 0.5 kg of peanuts

C2 To the nearest penny, work out
the cost of one fat treat.

Fat treats £1.30

C3 A pet shop sells wild bird food in bags.

Peanuts £2.56

Sunflower seed £4.53

Wild bird seed £2.97

Premium bird seed £5.64

(a) Work out the cost of a kilogram of peanuts.

(b) Work out the cost of a kilogram of seed for each bag.
Give your answers to the nearest penny.

13

D How much each?

26p

4 CREME EGGS £0.97

12 CREME EGGS £2.60

Use a calculator to answer these questions.

In this section, give your answers correct to the nearest penny.

D1 Supermarkets often sell crisps in large packs.

CRISPS
FAMILY PACK
6 PACKETS
£0.95

CRISPS
LARGE PACK
ASSORTED
12 PACKETS
£1.49

CRISPS
GIANT PACK
ASSORTED
18 PACKETS
£1.99

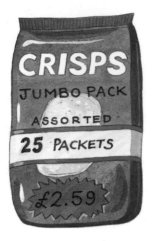

CRISPS
JUMBO PACK
ASSORTED
25 PACKETS
£2.59

(a) Work out the cost of a packet of crisps in each pack.

(b) What is the difference in cost of a packet of crisps in
the jumbo pack and in the family pack?

D2 A shop sells three kinds of eggs.

6 FREE RANGE
EGGS
£1.25

6 STANDARD
EGGS
£0.79

6 ECONOMY
EGGS
£0.39

(a) Find the cost of an egg in each pack.

(b) What is the difference in cost of one free range and one economy egg?

D3 What is the cost of a choc ice in each pack?

10 LIGHT
CHOC ICES
£0.19

6 Low Fat
CHOC ICES
£1.19

D4 (a) Find the cost of a pot of yoghurt in each pack.

(b) Which pack gives the cheapest pot of yoghurt?

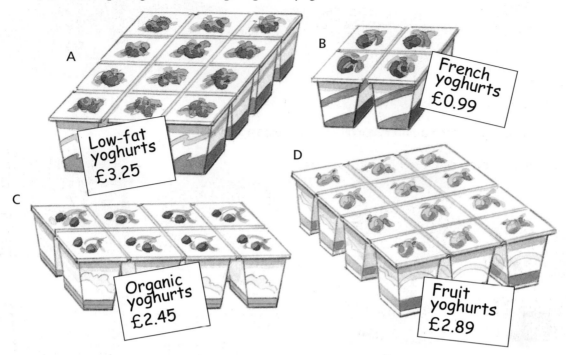

A Low-fat yoghurts £3.25

B French yoghurts £0.99

C Organic yoghurts £2.45

D Fruit yoghurts £2.89

D5 (a) Find the cost per kilogram of Basmati rice in each bag.

P 1kg £1.99

Q 2kg £3.79

R 4kg £6.99

(b) Find the cost per kilogram of long grain rice in these bags.

(c) Which is cheaper per kilogram, the long grain or the Basmati rice?

X ½kg £0.55

Y 4kg £3.69

E More for your money

Which box gives you
most for your money?

£0.60 0.3 kg

£0.90 0.5 kg

£2.00 1.2 kg

£3.99 3 kg

You may use a calculator in this section.

E1 (a) What is the cost per kilogram
for each box of grass seed?

A £2.99 0.25 kg

B £4.99 0.5 kg

C £8.99 1 kg

D £18.99 2 kg

(b) Which pack gives most seed for your money?

(c) Why might you prefer **not** to buy this pack?

E2 (a) Work out the cost per kilogram
for each bag of seaweed meal fertiliser.

(b) Which bag gives you most
for your money?

R

SEAWEED MEAL Fertilizer £27.75 25kg

P

SEAWEED MEAL Fertilizer £5.56 2.5kg

Q

SEAWEED MEAL Fertilizer £9.99 5kg

E3 (a) For each pack of slug killer, work out the cost per kilogram.

2 kg tub – £9.99   0.8 kg tub – £4.99   0.25 kg tub – £2.49

(b) Which pack gives you most for your money?

E4 Monkfield Ash garden centre sells a 5.5 kg bag of bone meal for £6.50.
St Paul's garden centre sells a 6 kg bag of bone meal for £10.45.

(a) Calculate the cost per kilogram of this bone meal from Monkfield Ash.

(b) Calculate the cost per kilogram of this bone meal from St Paul's.

(c) Which bag gives you more for your money?

E5 (a) A garden centre sells fish, blood
and bone fertiliser in boxes.

Find the cost per kilogram
for each box.

(b) A gardening catalogue sells the
same fish, blood and bone fertiliser.

Find the cost per kilogram for each bag.

(c) What is the cheapest way
to buy this fertiliser?

Fish, blood and bone
Ideal for use on a wide range of crops.

6 kg bag   £8.40
25 kg bag   £26.25

E6 A catalogue sells liquid seaweed extract
in five different amounts.

(a) Work out the cost per litre
for each amount.

(b) Derek needs 4 litres
of this seaweed extract.
What do you think is the
cheapest way for him to
buy his seaweed extract?

Seaweed extract

Highly concentrated, containing
natural plant growth stimulants and
an extensive range of trace elements.

0.125 litre   £2.10
0.5 litre   £4.99
1 litre   £7.99
5 litres   £22.49
25 litres   £94.50

What progress have you made?

Do not use a calculator in questions 1, 2 and 3.

Statement

I can solve simple money problems without a calculator.

I can solve problems with a calculator where I round to the nearest penny.

I know when to multiply and when to divide.

Evidence

1 A cup of coffee cost £0.84.
   What is the cost of 6 coffees?

2 A cup of tea costs 65p and a cake costs 34p.
   Find the cost of two teas and a cake.

3 Three friends decide to share the cost of a meal equally. The total cost is £47.85.
   How much does each friend pay?

4 Apples cost £1.69 per kilogram.
   To the nearest penny, find the cost of
   (a) 3.2 kg of apples   (b) 0.7 kg of apples

5 (a) 3 kg of potatoes cost £1.05.
        How much does 1 kg of potatoes cost?

   (b) Apples cost £1.05 a kilogram.
        How much do 3 kg of apples cost?

6 Work out the cost of a packet of crisps in each pack, correct to the nearest penny.

7 Find the cost of a kg of potatoes in each bag.

④ Making rules

This work will help you
- ◆ explore patterns and write down rules for them
- ◆ write formulas for rules
- ◆ draw graphs from simple rules
- ◆ draw and interpret graphs from real-life situations

A Rules with words

Good tea

This is a rule for making a pot of tea.

> *Good tea*
> *Use one spoonful for each person,*
> *and an extra spoonful for the pot.*

Tukutuku

These Maori women are weaving panels called tukutuku.

They are used to decorate the walls of their great houses in New Zealand.

This is a set of tukutuku patterns.

Pattern 1   Pattern 2   Pattern 3

- • How many crosses will there be in pattern 4?
- • How many crosses will there be in pattern 10?
- • How can you find the number of crosses from the pattern number?

A1 Look at these patterns.

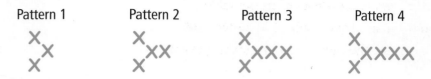

Pattern 1 Pattern 2 Pattern 3 Pattern 4

(a) Draw pattern 5 and pattern 6.

(b) Copy and complete this table.
It shows how many crosses there are in each pattern.

Pattern number	1	2	3	4	5	6
Number of crosses	3					

(c) How many crosses do you think there will be in pattern 10?
(Work it out without drawing.)

(d) How many crosses will there be in pattern 20?

(e) Which of these rules is correct?

Number of crosses = pattern number – 2

Number of crosses = pattern number + 1

Number of crosses = pattern number + 2

A2 (a) For the design below, draw patterns 5 and 6.

Pattern 1 Pattern 2 Pattern 3 Pattern 4

(b) Copy and complete this table.

Pattern number	1	2	3	4	5	6
Number of crosses	2					

(c) How many crosses will be in pattern 100?

(d) Work out a rule for the number of crosses in each pattern.

A3 Work out a rule for the number of crosses in these patterns.
If you need to, make your own table like the one in question A2.

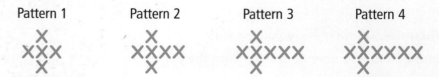

Pattern 1 Pattern 2 Pattern 3 Pattern 4

A4 Look at each of these designs. For each one
- make a *pattern number/number of crosses* table
- work out how many crosses will be in pattern 100
- work out a rule for the number of crosses in the patterns

A

Pattern 1	Pattern 2	Pattern 3	Pattern 4
XX	XX	XX	XX
XXX	XXXX	XXXXX	XXXXXX
XX	XX	XX	XX

B

Pattern 1	Pattern 2	Pattern 3	Pattern 4
X	XX	XXX	XXXX
X	X	X	X

C

Pattern 1	Pattern 2	Pattern 3	Pattern 4
XXX	XXXX	XXXXX	XXXXXX
XX	XXX	XXXX	XXXXX

D

Pattern 1	Pattern 2	Pattern 3	Pattern 4
X	XX	XXX	XXXX
XX X	XXX	XXXX	XXXXX
X	XX	XXX	XXXX

A5 John makes weak tea.

He uses half a spoonful for each person.

He does not put any in for the pot!

(a) How much tea would John use for 6 people?

(b) How much tea would he use for 8 people?

(c) John makes tea for 5 people.
How many spoonfuls does he use?

(d) Write the rule for John's tea. It connects the
number of spoonfuls and the *number of people*.

A6 Gold is being carried to the bank in armoured cars.
Each car has a motorbike on each side.
There is one motorbike at the front and one at the back.

(a) There are 4 armoured cars in the picture.
How many motorbikes are there?

(b) How many motorbikes would 5 armoured cars need?

(c) How many motorbikes would be needed for 6 cars?

(d) Without drawing, work out how many motorbikes
would be needed for 100 armoured cars.

(e) Write down the rule connecting the *number of motorbikes*
and the *number of cars*.

B Rules with letters

| *m* stands for the *number of matches* | *p* stands for the *pattern number* |

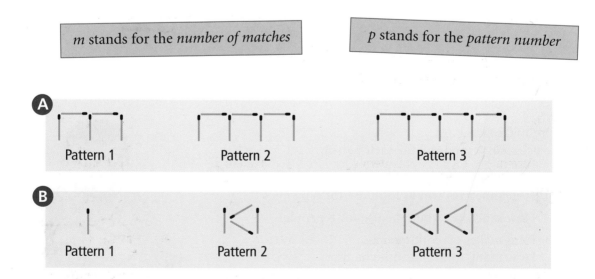

B1 Here is a set of patterns made with matches.

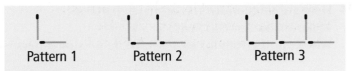

Pattern 1　　　　Pattern 2　　　　Pattern 3

(a) Draw pattern 4. How many matches does it use?

(b) Copy and complete this table.
(*p* stands for the *pattern number*,
m stands for the *number of matches*.)

p	1	2	3	4	5	6
m	3					

(c) Write a rule using words that says how many matches you need for each pattern number.

(d) Here are some rules using letters.
Which of these rules is the same as yours?

$p = m + 2$　　　$m = p + 2$　　　$p = 2m$　　　$m = 2p$

B2 Here is another set of match patterns.

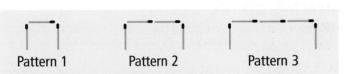

Pattern 1　　　　Pattern 2　　　　Pattern 3

(a) Make a table (like in question B1) for these patterns.

(b) Which of the rules below fits the patterns?

$p = m + 2$　　$m = p + 2$　　$p = 2m$　　$m = 3p$　　$m = 2p$

B3 Here are three rules.　　$m = 4p - 1$　　$m = 3p$　　$m = 2p + 1$

Below are three different sets of match patterns.

Which set goes with which rule?

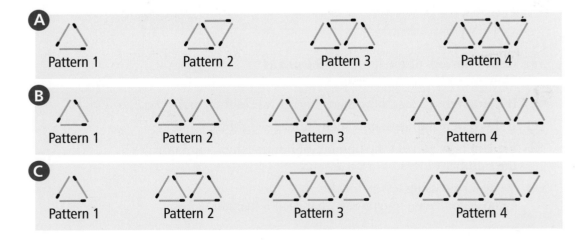

A Pattern 1　　Pattern 2　　Pattern 3　　Pattern 4

B Pattern 1　　Pattern 2　　Pattern 3　　Pattern 4

C Pattern 1　　Pattern 2　　Pattern 3　　Pattern 4

B4 Here are three more sets of match patterns.
Make a table for each set.
Work out the rule for each set. Write it using letters.

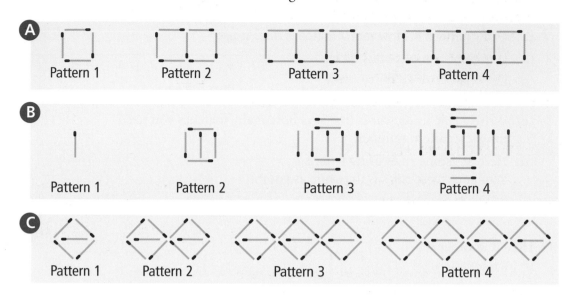

A

Pattern 1   Pattern 2   Pattern 3   Pattern 4

B

Pattern 1   Pattern 2   Pattern 3   Pattern 4

C

Pattern 1   Pattern 2   Pattern 3   Pattern 4

B5

(a) Count the legs of the horses in the picture.
How many horses are there?

(b) If there were 12 legs, how many horses would there be?

(c) If there were 100 legs, how many horses would there be?

(d) Explain how you get the number of horses when you know
the number of legs.

(e) Write a rule using letters for this.
Choose your own letters. Say what each letter stands for.

B6 Jay is drawing a set of matchstick patterns.
This is pattern 1 in his set of patterns.

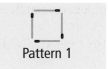

Pattern 1

The rule for his patterns is $m = 4p$.
m stands for the *number of matches,*
p stands for the *pattern number.*

(a) Work out m when $p = 2$.

(b) Draw pattern 2 to fit Jay's rule.

(c) Draw pattern 3. Check that it fits Jay's rule.

C Graphs from rules

Hasna is making patterns with matches.
Here are her first three patterns.

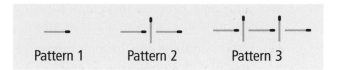

Pattern 1   Pattern 2   Pattern 3

- Copy and complete this table for Hasna's patterns.

Pattern number (p)	1	2	3	4	5
Number of matches (m)	1	3			

- Hasna thinks the rule for her pattern is $m = 2p - 1$.
  Check whether she is right.

- Use the rule to find the number of matches in pattern 10.

Hasna draws a graph from her table.
This shows part of her graph.

- Copy and complete this graph for
  Hasna's patterns.

- What do you notice about the points
  on the graph?

- Use your graph to find the number of
  matches in

  (a) pattern 7

  (b) pattern 12

Draw the patterns to check your answers.

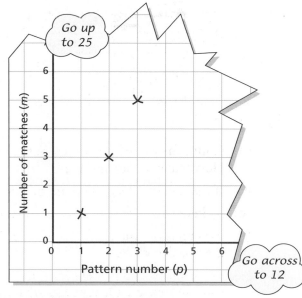

C1 Use your graph of Hasna's patterns to find the number of matches in

(a) pattern 6   (b) pattern 9   (c) pattern 11

C2 Look at these tukutuku patterns.

Pattern 1   **Pattern 2**   **Pattern 3**

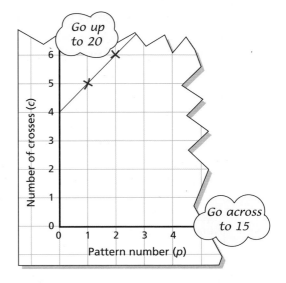

(a) Copy and complete this table.

Pattern number (p)	1	2	3	4	5
Number of crosses (c)	5	6			

(b) Work out a rule using letters for the number of crosses in each pattern.

(c) Use your rule to find the number of crosses in pattern 10.

(d) Copy and complete this graph showing the number of crosses in each pattern.

(e) Draw a straight line through the points. Extend your line across the graph.

(f) Use your graph to find the number of crosses in these patterns

   (i) pattern 7   (ii) pattern 13

C3 Caron is making patterns with nails.
The rule for her patterns is $n = 2p + 1$.

(a) Copy and complete this table for Caron's patterns.

Pattern number (p)	1	2	3	4	5
Number of nails (n)	3	5			

(b) How many nails are there in pattern 10?

(c) Draw a graph for Caron's rule.
Go up to pattern 12 on the horizontal scale.

(d) Use your graph to find the number of nails in

   (i) pattern 7   (ii) pattern 11

(e) What pattern number uses 19 nails?

C4 (a) For the rule $y = 3x - 2$, what will y be when

(i) $x = 2$ (ii) $x = 5$ (iii) $x = 9$

(b) Copy and complete this table for the rule $y = 3x - 2$.

x	1	2	3	4	5
$y = 3x - 2$	1				

(c) Draw a graph with the x-axis going from 0 to 9 and the y-axis going from 0 to 25.

(d) Plot the values from your table on the graph. Join the points up with a straight line. Label the line $y = 3x - 2$.

(e) Use your graph to find the value of y when $x = 7$. Check that this fits the rule.

C5 Coronet cars hire out expensive cars.
You can hire a stretch Cadillac from them.
The cost is   £30 to hire the car plus
              £2 for each mile travelled

Coronet Cars

Weddings • Tours • Theatre • Race days
• Picnics in style •

Impress your friends!

tel: (01233) 456000   www.coronetcars.co

(a) Copy and complete this table showing the distance travelled and cost.

Distance (miles)	10	20	30	50	100
Cost in £	50				

(b) Use your table to copy and complete this graph.

(c) Use your graph to find the cost if a Cadillac is hired and travels 70 miles.

(d) Dave hires a Cadillac. He has to pay £190. Use the graph to find how many miles he travelled.

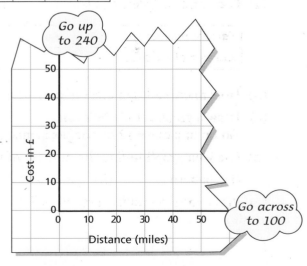

What progress have you made?

Statement

Evidence

I can work out a formula using words.

Pattern 1	Pattern 2	Pattern 3
X	X	X
XX	XXX	XXXX
X	X	X

1 (a) For the design above, sketch pattern 4 and pattern 5.

  (b) Copy and complete this table.

Pattern number	1	2	3	4	5
Number of crosses	4				

  (c) How many crosses would there be in pattern 10?

  (d) Work out a rule for the number of crosses in each pattern.

I can work out a formula which uses letters.

2 Here is a set of patterns made with matches.

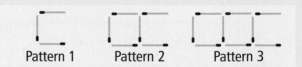

Pattern 1   Pattern 2   Pattern 3

  (a) Copy and complete this table.
      p stands for the *pattern number*.
      m stands for the *number of matches*.

p	1	2	3	4	5	6
m	3					

  (b) How many matches would there be in pattern 100?

  (c) Which of the rules below fits the patterns?

  $m = 3p$ $m = p + 3$

  $m = p + 2$ $m = 2p + 1$

I can draw a graph using a rule.

3 (a) Complete this table for $y = 2x + 3$.

x	1	2	3	4	10
$y = 2x + 3$	5				

  (b) Draw a graph for this rule.

⑤ Fractions

This work will help you
- ◆ calculate a fraction of a number
- ◆ simplify fractions
- ◆ add and subtract simple fractions

A Seeing fractions

This square is split into 3 parts.

Is $\frac{1}{3}$ of the square shaded red?

Part of each shape is shaded red – but is it the fraction that it says?

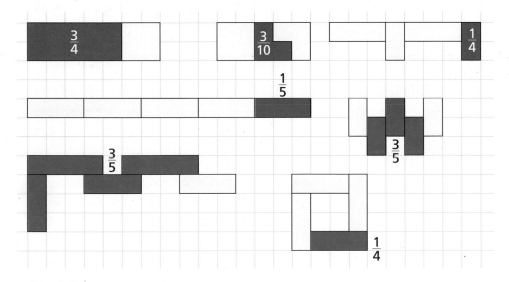

A1 For each of these say
- what fraction is red
- what fraction is yellow

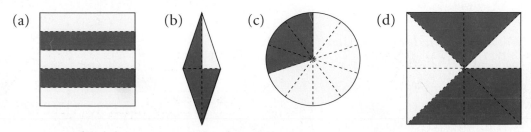

(a) (b) (c) (d)

A2 (a) Draw a square. Shade $\frac{3}{4}$ of it.

(b) Draw another square. Shade $\frac{3}{4}$ in a different way.

A3 The dot is $\frac{3}{4}$ of the way along the line from this end.

Roughly how far along the line from this end is each dot?

(a) ————————————————

(b) ————————————————

(c) ————————————————

(d) ————————————————

B Fractions of amounts

$\frac{1}{4}$ of 12   ●●●|○○○|○○○|○○○   is 12 ÷ 4 = **3**.

$\frac{1}{5}$ of 20   ●●●●|○○○○|○○○○|○○○○|○○○○   is 20 ÷ 5 = **4**.

$\frac{2}{5}$ of 20   ●●●●|●●●●|○○○○|○○○○|○○○○   is 2 × 4 = **8**.

B1 Match each statement below with one of the diagrams.

| $\frac{1}{4}$ of 20 = 5 | $\frac{1}{10}$ of 30 = 3 | $\frac{1}{2}$ of 10 = 5 | $\frac{1}{5}$ of 10 = 2 | $\frac{1}{5}$ of 15 = 3 | $\frac{1}{3}$ of 15 = 5 |

A ● ● ● ● ●   B ○ ○ ○ ○ ○   C ● ○ ○ ○ ○ ○ ○ ○ ○ ○
  ○ ○ ○ ○ ○   ○ ○ ○ ○ ○   ● ○ ○ ○ ○ ○ ○ ○ ○ ○
  ○ ○ ○ ○ ○   ● ● ● ● ●   ● ○ ○ ○ ○ ○ ○ ○ ○ ○
                       ○ ○ ○ ○ ○

D ○ ○ ○ ○ ●   E ○ ○ ○ ○ ●   F ○ ○ ○ ○ ○
  ○ ○ ○ ○ ●   ○ ○ ○ ○ ●   ● ● ● ● ●
  ○ ○ ○ ○ ●

B2 Work these out, using diagrams if you need to.

(a) $\frac{1}{4}$ of 8   (b) $\frac{1}{3}$ of 12   (c) $\frac{1}{5}$ of 20   (d) $\frac{1}{4}$ of 24   (e) $\frac{1}{7}$ of 42

(f) $\frac{1}{2}$ of 18   (g) $\frac{1}{4}$ of 36   (h) $\frac{1}{5}$ of 35   (i) $\frac{1}{10}$ of 60   (j) $\frac{1}{4}$ of 40

(k) $\frac{1}{2}$ of 90   (l) $\frac{1}{3}$ of 63   (m) $\frac{1}{4}$ of 64   (n) $\frac{1}{10}$ of 30   (o) $\frac{1}{10}$ of 200

B3 Match each statement below with one of the diagrams.

$\frac{3}{4}$ of 16 = 12

$\frac{2}{3}$ of 15 = 10

$\frac{3}{5}$ of 25 = 15

$\frac{2}{5}$ of 25 = 10

$\frac{3}{5}$ of 20 = 12

$\frac{3}{4}$ of 20 = 15

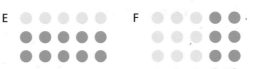

B4 Work these out.

(a) $\frac{3}{4}$ of 36   (b) $\frac{3}{5}$ of 40   (c) $\frac{3}{10}$ of 50   (d) $\frac{2}{3}$ of 21

(e) $\frac{4}{5}$ of 25   (f) $\frac{5}{6}$ of 42   (g) $\frac{3}{7}$ of 35   (h) $\frac{6}{10}$ of 80

For questions B5 to B11 you may need a calculator.

B5 Work these out.

(a) $\frac{1}{2}$ of 1372   (b) $\frac{1}{4}$ of 2252   (c) $\frac{1}{3}$ of 12 714

(d) $\frac{1}{10}$ of 46 030   (e) $\frac{1}{5}$ of 327 185   (f) $\frac{1}{4}$ of 14 788

B6 In 1998 the Northern Ireland Assembly was set up with 108 seats.
$\frac{1}{6}$ of those elected were from the Sinn Fein party.
How many of those elected were from Sinn Fein?

B7 In 1993 a large sheep station in Australia had 127 404 sheep.
$\frac{1}{3}$ of them were black. How many of these sheep were black?

B8 A large hanging basket was once made with 600 plants.
$\frac{1}{10}$ of the plants had pink flowers.

How many of the plants had pink flowers?

B9 Work these out.

(a) $\frac{2}{3}$ of 222   (b) $\frac{3}{4}$ of 340   (c) $\frac{7}{10}$ of 7110   (d) $\frac{2}{5}$ of 2115

B10 In Canada in 1983 a Bingo session had 15 755 people taking part.
$\frac{3}{5}$ of these were women.

How many of those taking part were women?

B11 A very long zip-fastener was once made with 2 565 900 teeth.
If $\frac{7}{10}$ of the teeth were closed, how many teeth were open?

C Equivalent fractions

What fraction does each of these diagrams show?

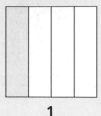 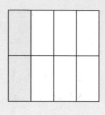 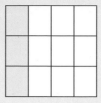 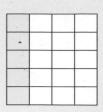

$\dfrac{1}{4}$ $\dfrac{}{8}$ $-$ $-$

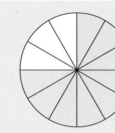

$\dfrac{3}{4} = \dfrac{9}{12}$ ×3 ×3

$\dfrac{3}{4}$ and $\dfrac{9}{12}$ are **equivalent fractions**.

C1 Use these diagrams to complete the equivalent fractions below.

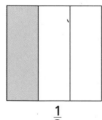 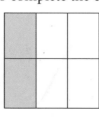 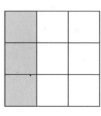 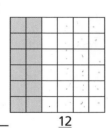

$\dfrac{1}{3} = \dfrac{}{6} = \dfrac{}{9} = \dfrac{}{12}$

C2 Copy and complete these equivalent fractions.

(a) $\dfrac{1}{5} = \dfrac{}{10}$ (b) $\dfrac{1}{7} = \dfrac{2}{}$ (c) $\dfrac{1}{4} = \dfrac{}{12}$ (d) $\dfrac{1}{2} = \dfrac{6}{}$

(e) $\dfrac{2}{5} = \dfrac{}{15}$ (f) $\dfrac{3}{7} = \dfrac{}{21}$ (g) $\dfrac{5}{12} = \dfrac{20}{}$ (h) $\dfrac{3}{4} = \dfrac{}{24}$

C3 Copy and complete these equivalent fractions.

(a) $\dfrac{1}{5} = \dfrac{}{15} = \dfrac{}{30}$ (b) $\dfrac{3}{4} = \dfrac{}{16} = \dfrac{}{20}$

(c) $\dfrac{2}{3} = \dfrac{}{9} = \dfrac{}{12} = \dfrac{14}{}$ (d) $\dfrac{5}{6} = \dfrac{}{12} = \dfrac{25}{} = \dfrac{}{18}$

C4 Write down four different fractions that are equivalent to $\dfrac{3}{5}$.

C5 Write down four different fractions that are equivalent to $\dfrac{5}{8}$.

C6 Draw a diagram to show how many $\dfrac{1}{8}$s there are in $\dfrac{3}{4}$.

C7 Draw a diagram to show how many $\dfrac{1}{12}$s there are in $\dfrac{2}{3}$.

You can simplify a fraction by dividing the numerator (top) and denominator (bottom) by the same number.

For example

If you cannot simplify any further, the fraction is in its **simplest form**.

C8 Simplify each of these fractions.

(a) $\frac{8}{10}$ (b) $\frac{6}{8}$ (c) $\frac{2}{4}$ (d) $\frac{70}{100}$ (e) $\frac{6}{10}$

C9 Write each of these fractions in the simplest possible way.

(a) $\frac{2}{6}$ (b) $\frac{6}{12}$ (c) $\frac{9}{12}$ (d) $\frac{60}{100}$ (e) $\frac{15}{20}$

C10 What fraction of this strip has been shaded?
Write it in its simplest form.

C11 What fraction of this row of beads is blue?
Write the fraction in its simplest form.

C12 Write each of these fractions in its simplest form.

(a) The fraction of cans open

(b) The fraction of eggs broken

(c) The fraction of CD cases empty

C13 There are 30 children in class 4S and 18 of them are absent with flu.
What fraction of the class is absent? Write it in its simplest form.

C14 Jack has 40 stamps.
25 are British, 10 are French and the rest are American.
What fraction, in its simplest form, of his stamps are

(a) British (b) French (c) American

C15 This diagram shows that the improper fraction $\frac{7}{4}$ is equivalent to the mixed number $1\frac{3}{4}$.

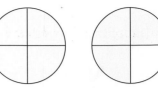

Write down the mixed number equivalent to each of these improper fractions.

(a) $\frac{9}{4}$ (b) $\frac{8}{5}$ (c) $\frac{11}{6}$ (d) $\frac{13}{4}$ (e) $\frac{22}{5}$

(f) $\frac{16}{7}$ (g) $\frac{23}{10}$ (h) $\frac{31}{5}$ (i) $\frac{57}{10}$ (j) $\frac{42}{8}$

C16 Write these mixed numbers as an equivalent improper fraction.

(a) $2\frac{1}{2}$ (b) $3\frac{2}{3}$ (c) $3\frac{2}{5}$ (d) $2\frac{3}{7}$ (e) $3\frac{4}{5}$

(f) $3\frac{3}{8}$ (g) $5\frac{1}{3}$ (h) $7\frac{3}{5}$ (i) $4\frac{2}{9}$ (j) $6\frac{1}{12}$

D Adding and subtracting fractions

This shows that $\frac{3}{7} + \frac{2}{7} = \frac{5}{7}$.

This shows that $\frac{7}{10} - \frac{4}{10} = \frac{3}{10}$.

D1 Draw a diagram to show that $\frac{2}{9} + \frac{5}{9} = \frac{7}{9}$

D2 Work these out.

(a) $\frac{1}{5} + \frac{2}{5}$ (b) $\frac{1}{3} + \frac{1}{3}$ (c) $\frac{2}{11} + \frac{3}{11}$ (d) $\frac{5}{9} + \frac{3}{9}$

(e) $\frac{4}{7} + \frac{2}{7}$ (f) $\frac{1}{12} + \frac{4}{12}$ (g) $\frac{3}{8} + \frac{2}{8}$ (h) $\frac{4}{13} + \frac{5}{13}$

D3 Work out these additions.
Write each answer in its simplest form.

(a) $\frac{3}{8} + \frac{1}{8}$ (b) $\frac{3}{8} + \frac{3}{8}$ (c) $\frac{3}{12} + \frac{5}{12}$ (d) $\frac{2}{9} + \frac{4}{9}$

(e) $\frac{4}{12} + \frac{5}{12}$ (f) $\frac{1}{12} + \frac{5}{12}$ (g) $\frac{3}{15} + \frac{6}{15}$ (h) $\frac{1}{9} + \frac{2}{9}$

D4 Work these out.

(a) $\frac{7}{9} - \frac{2}{9}$ (b) $\frac{2}{3} - \frac{1}{3}$ (c) $\frac{7}{11} - \frac{3}{11}$ (d) $\frac{5}{9} - \frac{1}{9}$

(e) $\frac{7}{8} - \frac{4}{8}$ (f) $\frac{9}{12} - \frac{4}{12}$ (g) $\frac{3}{8} - \frac{2}{8}$ (h) $\frac{8}{9} - \frac{7}{9}$

D5 Work out these subtractions.
Write each answer in its simplest form.

(a) $\frac{7}{8} - \frac{3}{8}$ (b) $\frac{5}{9} - \frac{2}{9}$ (c) $\frac{11}{12} - \frac{5}{12}$ (d) $\frac{5}{6} - \frac{2}{6}$

(e) $\frac{5}{8} - \frac{3}{8}$ (f) $\frac{11}{12} - \frac{1}{12}$ (g) $\frac{13}{16} - \frac{9}{16}$ (h) $\frac{10}{24} - \frac{1}{24}$

D6 This diagram shows that $\frac{1}{4} + \frac{1}{8} = \frac{3}{8}$.

Write an addition sum for each of these diagrams.

(a)   (b)   (c)

D7 Work these out.

(a) $\frac{1}{2} + \frac{3}{8}$ (b) $\frac{1}{4} + \frac{3}{8}$ (c) $\frac{1}{4} + \frac{5}{8}$

*D8 Look at these two circles.

(a) What fraction of a circle is shaded green?

(b) What fraction of a circle is shaded yellow?

(c) What fraction of a circle is shaded either green or yellow?
Write your answer as a mixed number.

*D9 Work these out.

(a) $\frac{1}{2} + \frac{5}{8}$ (b) $\frac{3}{4} + \frac{5}{8}$ (c) $1\frac{1}{2} + \frac{3}{4}$

What progress have you made?

Statement	Evidence

I can work out a fraction of a number.

1 Work these out.

(a) $\frac{1}{4}$ of 12   (b) $\frac{1}{5}$ of 45

2 Work these out.

(a) $\frac{3}{4}$ of 40   (b) $\frac{7}{10}$ of 30

I can simplify fractions.

3 Simplify these.

(a) $\frac{40}{100}$ (b) $\frac{14}{20}$

4 Write each fraction in the simplest way.

(a) $\frac{16}{20}$ (b) $\frac{80}{100}$ (c) $\frac{6}{30}$ (d) $\frac{16}{24}$

I can add and subtract simple fractions.

5 Work these out and, where possible, simplify.

(a) $\frac{1}{5} + \frac{3}{5}$ (b) $\frac{7}{11} + \frac{3}{11}$ (c) $\frac{3}{12} + \frac{5}{12}$

(d) $\frac{4}{5} - \frac{3}{5}$ (e) $\frac{6}{7} - \frac{2}{7}$ (f) $\frac{7}{8} - \frac{1}{8}$

35

Review 1

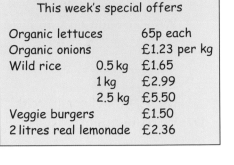

GREEN'S WHOLEFOODS

This week's special offers

Organic lettuces	65p each
Organic onions	£1.23 per kg
Wild rice	0.5 kg	£1.65
	1 kg	£2.99
	2.5 kg	£5.50
Veggie burgers	£1.50
2 litres real lemonade	£2.36

1 This poster shows some things for sale at a shop.

Use a calculator in these questions and round your answers to the nearest penny.

(a) Find the cost of an organic lettuce, 2 litres of real lemonade and a 0.5 kg bag of wild rice.

(b) Find the cost of three organic lettuces.

(c) Find the cost of 1.4 kg of organic onions.

(d) There are 6 burgers in a packet of veggie burgers. How much does each burger cost?

(e) Find the cost per kilogram of each of the bags of wild rice. Which size bag is cheaper per kilogram?

2 Use a calculator to answer these questions.

(a) 27 408 fans attended a World Cup football match. $\frac{1}{4}$ of them were English fans. How many fans were English?

(b) A nursery sows 1170 pepper seeds. They expect $\frac{4}{5}$ of them to grow into plants they can sell. How many plants can they expect to have to sell?

3 There are 32 children in class 9M and 20 of them go on a school trip. What fraction of the class go on the trip? Write the fraction in its simplest form.

4 Eight points are equally spaced around a circle. The points are numbered 1 to 8. The points can be joined up in order to give different shapes. The diagram shows a 2, 6, 8 triangle.

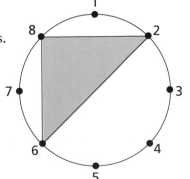

(a) What special type of triangle is the 2, 6, 8 triangle?

(b) What special type of triangle is a 2, 5, 7 triangle?

(c) Find three different numbers which join up to give a triangle which is congruent to the 2, 5, 7 triangle.

(d) What special type of quadrilateral do you get by joining the numbers 1, 3, 4, 8?

(e) What special type of quadrilateral do you get by joining the numbers 3, 6, 7, 8?

5 Write these fractions as mixed numbers.

(a) $\frac{7}{4}$ (b) $\frac{13}{6}$ (c) $\frac{17}{5}$ (d) $\frac{27}{6}$

6 Nasima is making patterns with matches.
Here are her first three patterns.

Pattern 1   Pattern 2   Pattern 3

(a) Copy and complete this table for
Nasima's patterns.

Pattern number (p)	1	2	3	4	5
Number of matches (m)	4	6			

(b) Which of these is the correct rule for Nasima's pattern?

$m = 4p$ $m = 2p - 2$ $m = 2p$

$m = 2p + 2$ $m = p + 2$

(c) Use the rule to find the number of matches
in pattern 10.

(d) Copy and complete this graph showing
the number of matches in each pattern.

(e) Draw a straight line through the points.
Extend your line across the graph.

(f) Use your graph to find what pattern number
uses 18 matches.

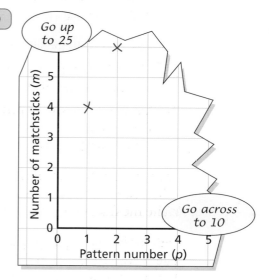

Go up to 25

Go across to 10

Number of matchsticks (m)

Pattern number (p)

7 Write each of these in their simplest form.

(a) The fraction of the cola bottles
that are empty

(b) The fraction of the beans that
are sprouting

8 Work these out, writing each answer in its simplest form.

(a) $\frac{2}{11} + \frac{6}{11}$ (b) $\frac{5}{9} + \frac{2}{9}$ (c) $\frac{5}{8} - \frac{2}{8}$ (d) $\frac{7}{12} - \frac{5}{12}$

⑥ Probability

This work will help you

◆ use probability to help make choices

◆ use fractions to write the probability of events happening

◆ compare probabilities using fractions

A Your choice!

Up or down   a game for two players

You need cards numbered 1 to 5 turned face down.

• The first player turns over one card.

• The other player then guesses whether the card they pick next will be higher or lower.

• They now turn over a card. If their guess is correct they win one point.

• The cards are shuffled and laid face down again.
  Players take it in turns to be the first player.

• The first person to get 10 points wins.

Higher or lower   a game for two players

You need a set of cards numbered 1 to 9.

• Shuffle the cards and put them in a line face down.

• Turn over the first card.

• Guess whether the second card is higher or lower.
  It may help to make a list from 1 to 9.   1 2 3 4 5 6 ⑦ 8 9

• Turn it over. If your guess is correct you win a point.

• Now the other player guesses whether the third card will be
  higher or lower than the second card.

Carry on like this, taking turns to guess.   1 2 ③ 4 5 6 ✗ 8 9
When all the cards have been turned over, shuffle them and start again.

The first person with 10 points is the winner.

A1 If you were playing 'Up or down', would you say 'higher' or 'lower' if your partner turned over

(a) a 4   (b) a 2   (c) a 5

A2 (a) Is there any first card which would make you certain about your choice?

(b) What first card gives you an even chance of winning or losing?

A3 Here are some unfinished 'Higher or lower' games.
If it was your turn to go, would you say 'higher' or 'lower'?

(a) 6 9 7 5

(b) 5 1 7 3

(c) 5 6 4 9

(d) 9 6 5 4

(e) 1 4 8 3 6

A4 Here are three unfinished 'Higher or lower' games, A, B and C.

Which one of these three games gives the best chance of 'higher'?
Explain your choice.

A 7 2 4 8 6

B 6 5 8

C 7 9 6 5

B Using fractions

In this game a marble is placed under one cup. The cups are 'shuffled' and the player has to guess which cup the marble is under.

1 out of 3 (one third) of the cups have a marble underneath.
There is one chance out of three of picking the cup with the marble underneath.

We say that the probability of picking the cup with the marble underneath is $\frac{1}{3}$.

Here the probability of picking a cup with a marble underneath is two out of seven chances or $\frac{2}{7}$.

Two of these have a marble underneath.

B1 Here are some 'Find the marble' games.
For each one write down the probability (chance) of finding a marble.

(a)   (b)

(c)   (d)

B2 Write down the probability of finding a marble in each of these games.

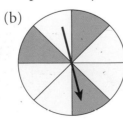   (a)   (b)   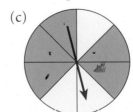   (c)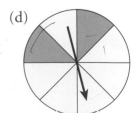

B3 What can you say about the chance of finding a marble in each part of question B2?

B4 Look at the spinners below.
For each one, what is the probability of blue winning?

(a)   (b)   (c)   (d)

B5 A spinner is divided into equal parts.
6 parts are blue; the other 4 parts are yellow.

(a) What is the probability of blue winning?

(b) What is the probability of yellow winning?

If we do something in a game or activity without knowing what
will happen, we say that it is **at random**.

Choosing something 'without looking' is at random.

B6 A box contains 12 pens. Only 7 of the pens work.
A pen is taken out at random (without looking).

(a) What is the probability of choosing a pen that works?

(b) What is the probability of choosing a pen that doesn't work?

(c) Which has the greater chance of being chosen, a pen that works
or one that doesn't?

B7 The names of Anne, Brian, Carol, David and Edward are
written on separate scraps of paper.
The scraps are placed in a box and one is taken out at random.

(a) How many scraps of paper are there?

(b) What is the probability of a boy's name being chosen?

(c) What is the probability of a girl's name being chosen?

B8 A box contains 6 blue pens, 4 black pens and 2 red pens.
A pen is taken from the box without looking.

(a) How many pens are there altogether?

(b) What is the probability of a blue pen being chosen?

(c) What is the probability of a black pen being chosen?

(d) What is the probability of a red pen being chosen?

B9 In class 9C there are 12 boys and 16 girls.
Their names are put on a list and one name is chosen at random.

(a) How many pupils are there in the class altogether?

(b) What is the probability of a boy being chosen?

(c) What is the probability of a girl being chosen?

B10 Look at the spinner on the right.

(a) What is the probability of red winning?

(b) What is the probability of blue winning?

(c) What is the probability of yellow winning?

(d) Look at the probability line below.
Each letter shows the probability of a colour winning.
Which letter stands for each colour?

C Comparing fractions

You need sheet 269.

Fraction boxes

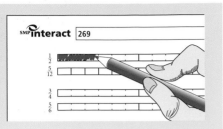

On the sheet, shade $\frac{1}{2}$ of the top fraction box.
Shade $\frac{5}{12}$ of the fraction box below it.

Which is bigger, $\frac{1}{2}$ or $\frac{5}{12}$?

Shade the next two boxes to decide which is bigger, $\frac{3}{4}$ or $\frac{5}{6}$.

C1 (a) Shade $\frac{3}{4}$ of the box for part (a).

　　(b) Shade $\frac{2}{3}$ of the next box.

　　(c) Which is bigger, $\frac{3}{4}$ or $\frac{2}{3}$?

C2 Shade fraction boxes to find out which is greater in each of these pairs of fractions.

　　(a) $\frac{7}{12}$ and $\frac{1}{2}$　　　　(b) $\frac{9}{12}$ and $\frac{5}{6}$　　　　(c) $\frac{8}{12}$ and $\frac{2}{3}$

C3 Use the sheet to help you put these fractions in order of size, starting with the smallest one.　$\frac{1}{4}$　$\frac{1}{6}$　$\frac{4}{12}$

Fractions which are the same size but have different numbers in them are called **equivalent fractions**.

For example, these three fractions are all equivalent.

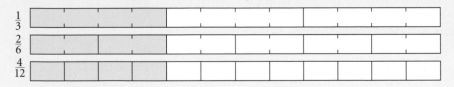

C4 Here are two 'Find the marble' games.

　　In which game, A or B, do you have the bigger chance of finding a marble?
Explain.

C5 Use sheet 269 to find two fractions equivalent to $\frac{2}{3}$.

C6 Use your answer to question C5 to draw two different marble games which both give the same chance of finding a marble.

A better chance?

On which of these two games do you have a better chance of winning?
How can you tell?

Lost your marbles?
There are 3 hidden
under these cups!

Find the marble!
There are 5 hidden
under these cups!

C7 For each of these marble finding games, write down

- the probability of winning for A and for B

- whether A or B gives the greater chance of finding the marble.
  (If it is the same chance then write 'same'.)

(a) A    B

(b) A    B

(c) A   B

(d) A   B

C8 For each pair of bags, work out which bag gives you the better chance
of picking a blue counter.
If both bags have the same chance, write 'same'.

(a)   (b)

(c)   (d)

(a)   (b)

C9 Shuna's favourite flavour sweet is lime.
She has to choose a sweet without looking from one of the boxes
in each of the pairs below.
Which box in each pair gives her the greater chance of choosing lime?

(a) Box X has 7 lime and 5 orange.   Box Y has 2 lime and 2 orange.

(b) Box P has 5 lime and 1 lemon.   Box Q has 11 lime and 1 lemon.

(c) Box M has 4 lime and 2 banana.   Box N has 9 lime and 3 banana.

What progress have you made?

Statement

Evidence

I can choose which of two things is more likely to happen.

1 Five cards numbered 1, 2, 3, 4 and 5 are shuffled and placed face down in a row.

Is the second card more likely to be higher or lower if the first card was

(a) 4   (b) 1   (c) 3

I can write probabilities as fractions.

2 Write down the probability of

(a) choosing a cup with a marble under it from these

(b) choosing a red counter, without looking, from this bag

(c) choosing a cherry flavour sweet from a bag with 7 cherry flavour and 5 orange

I can compare probabilities using fractions.

3 Which of these bags gives you the greater chance of choosing a blue counter? (Use sheet 269 if you want.)

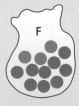
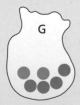

4 In which of these boxes do you have a greater probability of choosing a blue pen at random?

Box A: 5 blue pens and 7 red pens

Box B: 3 blue pens and 3 red pens

⑦ Earning money

This work will help you use hourly rates of pay

COLLEGE *of technology*

Cleaners wanted
£5.75 p/h.
Transport provided
Tel: 01212 765433?

CLEANER Tues and Fri
6pm - 8pm.
£22.20 per week.
Tel: 01212 5324765.

MORNING CLEANER
Mon - Fri 7.30 - 9.30am
£58.50 p/w
Tel: 01212 5324822

FULL-TIME CLEANER reqd
£10,465 pa. 35 hpw.
Contact Mrs Walton on 01212 67342?1.

1 Ken is a sales assistant in a chocolate shop. He earns £4.90 per hour.
How much does he earn for a 38 hour week?

2 Sarah is an HGV driver. One week she works 42.5 hours and earns £276.25.
What is her hourly rate of pay?

3 Work out the weekly wage for each of these jobs.

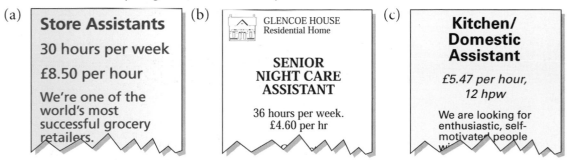

(a)
Store Assistants

30 hours per week

£8.50 per hour

We're one of the
world's most
successful grocery
retailers.

(b)
GLENCOE HOUSE
Residential Home

**SENIOR
NIGHT CARE
ASSISTANT**

36 hours per week.
£4.60 per hr

(c)
**Kitchen/
Domestic
Assistant**

*£5.47 per hour,
12 hpw*

We are looking for
enthusiastic, self-
motivated people

4 Diane works as a domestic assistant in a hospital.
She earns £170.86 for a 35.5 hour week.
What is her hourly rate of pay, correct to the nearest penny?

5 For each of these jobs, work out the hourly rate of pay,
correct to the nearest penny.

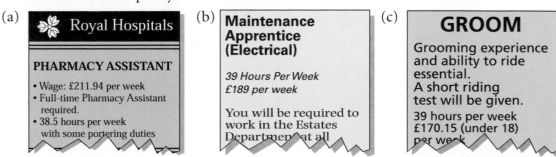

(a)
❀ Royal Hospitals

PHARMACY ASSISTANT

• Wage: £211.94 per week
• Full-time Pharmacy Assistant
  required.
• 38.5 hours per week
  with some portering duties

(b)
**Maintenance
Apprentice
(Electrical)**

*39 Hours Per Week
£189 per week*

You will be required to
work in the Estates
Department at all

(c)
GROOM

Grooming experience
and ability to ride
essential.
A short riding
test will be given.

39 hours per week
£170.15 (under 18)
per week

6 Peter earns £12 646 per year as a community support worker for the homeless. He works for 37.5 hours each week.

(a) Peter is paid for 52 weeks. How much does Peter earn in one week?

(b) Find his hourly rate of pay, correct to the nearest penny.

7 For each of these jobs, calculate:

- the amount earned in a week
- the hourly rate of pay

(a)
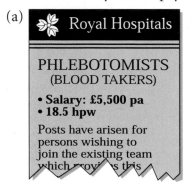

Royal Hospitals

PHLEBOTOMISTS
(BLOOD TAKERS)

• **Salary: £5,500 pa**
• **18.5 hpw**

Posts have arisen for persons wishing to join the existing team which provides this

(b)
Librarian

Commencing salary
£16,394 pa

Working 36.7 hours per week, you will have responsibility for the management of the Abbey View Learning Resource Centre

(c)
CARBY SCHOOL

LABORATORY TECHNICIAN

£13,400 per annum (36.7 h.p.w.)

We are seeking to appoint a Laboratory Technician to support

(d)
Early years & Childcare Development Manager

£29661 pa

This is a unique opportunity to lead the development of a new service designed to ensure that quality early years education is available to all children who need it. You will work 37 hours per week based at County Hall in Shrewsbury. You will have a

(e)
HIGH HILL TRUST

Community Nursing Liaison - R.G.N.

Hours: 22.5

Salary: £12,060

Car driver: Essential

An opportunity has arisen for an enthusiastic person with a good type of

8 Which of these three jobs pays the best hourly rate?

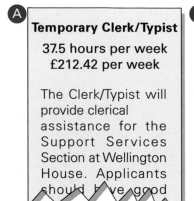

A

Temporary Clerk/Typist

37.5 hours per week
£212.42 per week

The Clerk/Typist will provide clerical assistance for the Support Services Section at Wellington House. Applicants should have good

B Switchboard operator

£5542.68 pa to work
18.5 hours per week

At least 12 months experience of working on a modern switchboard within a large organisation is essential for the post. You must have a helpful courteous disposition and be able to

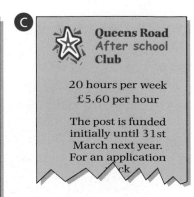

C **Queens Road After school Club**

20 hours per week
£5.60 per hour

The post is funded initially until 31st March next year. For an application

Garden centre

This work will help you with mental arithmetic.

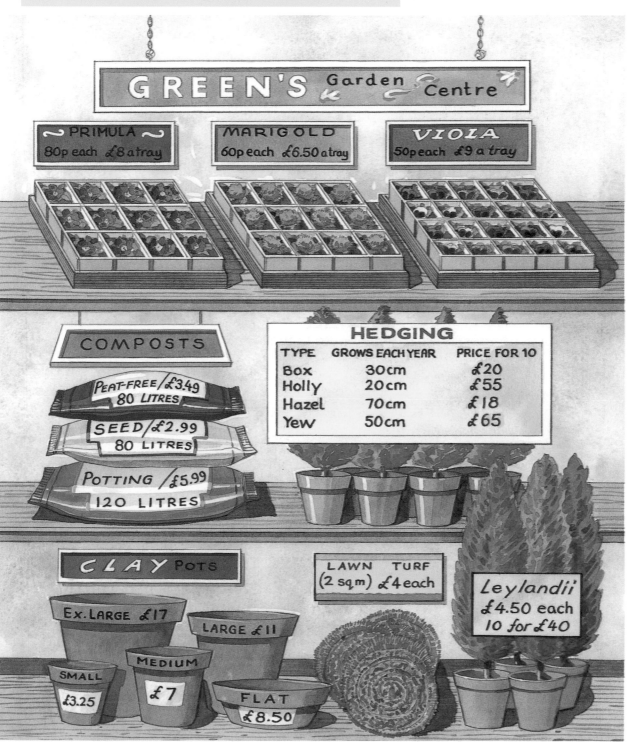

GREEN'S Garden Centre

~ PRIMULA ~
80p each £8 a tray

MARIGOLD
60p each £6.50 a tray

VIOLA
50p each £9 a tray

COMPOSTS

PEAT-FREE £3.49
80 LITRES

SEED £2.99
80 LITRES

POTTING £5.99
120 LITRES

HEDGING

TYPE	GROWS EACH YEAR	PRICE FOR 10
Box	30cm	£20
Holly	20cm	£55
Hazel	70cm	£18
Yew	50cm	£65

CLAY POTS

Ex.LARGE £17

LARGE £11

MEDIUM £7

SMALL £3.25

FLAT £8.50

LAWN TURF
(2 sq m) £4 each

Leylandii
£4.50 each
10 for £40

⑨ Percentages

This work will help you work out percentages of quantities

A 50 per cent

What is ...?

| half of 18 | $\frac{1}{2}$ of £40 | $\frac{1}{2}$ of 12 | $\frac{1}{2}$ of 20 |

$\frac{1}{2}$ of 10

a half of £28 $\frac{1}{2}$ of 30 $\frac{1}{2}$ of 60 cm $\frac{1}{2}$ of £70

Charts

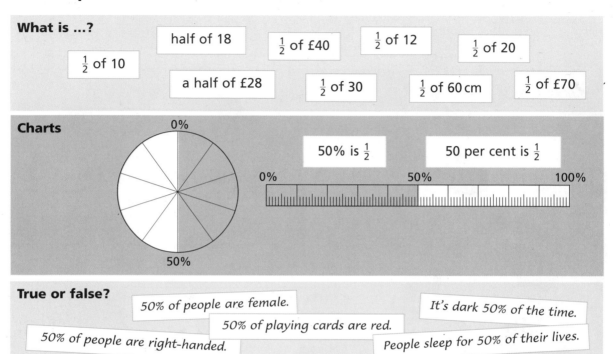

50% is $\frac{1}{2}$

50 per cent is $\frac{1}{2}$

True or false?

 50% of people are female.

50% of playing cards are red.

 It's dark 50% of the time.

50% of people are right-handed.

People sleep for 50% of their lives.

A1 Find a half of

(a) 8   (b) 18   (c) 200   (d) 46   (e) 480   (f) 9

A2 What is $\frac{1}{2}$ of

(a) £6   (b) £7   (c) 50 cm   (d) 440 g   (e) 3 m   (f) £140

A3 In which of these diagrams is 50% shaded red?

A   B   C   D

A4 Find 50% of

(a) 14   (b) £10   (c) 40 cm   (d) 300   (e) £50   (f) 32p

(g) £6.04   (h) 108   (i) 5 m   (j) £15   (k) 212 cm   (l) 660 g

B 25 per cent

Charts

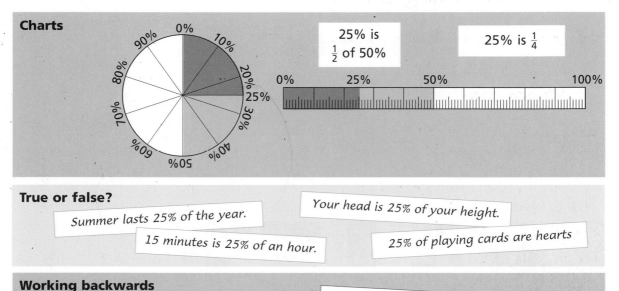

25% is $\frac{1}{2}$ of 50%

25% is $\frac{1}{4}$

True or false?

Summer lasts 25% of the year.

Your head is 25% of your height.

15 minutes is 25% of an hour.

25% of playing cards are hearts

Working backwards

25% of my friends wear glasses.
I have 6 friends with glasses.

I spend 25% of my pocket money on sweets.
This week I spent £1.50 on sweets.

B1 In which of these diagrams is 25% shaded red?

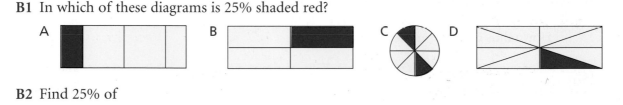

B2 Find 25% of

    (a) 16   (b) 40   (c) 12 m   (d) 200 g   (e) £240   (f) £10

B3 Raj wins £600. He gives 25% of it to his mum.
How much does he give to his mum?

B4 Emma wins £800. She keeps 50%.
She gives 25% to her Aunty Flo and the rest to her brother.

    (a) How much does Emma keep for herself?

    (b) How much does Aunty Flo get?

    (c) How much does her brother get?

B5 Jo won some money. She gave 25% to her dad.
She gave her dad £30. How much did Jo win?

B6 I think of a number. 25% of my number is 8.
What number am I thinking of?

B7 25% of the pupils in Karl's class have flu. 7 pupils have flu.
How many pupils are there altogether in Karl's class?

C 75 per cent

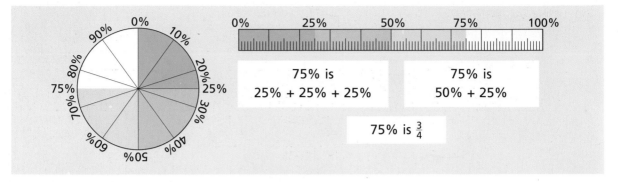

75% is
25% + 25% + 25%

75% is
50% + 25%

75% is $\frac{3}{4}$

C1 In which of these diagrams is 75% shaded red?

C2 Find 75% of

(a) 20   (b) £4   (c) £100   (d) 12 m   (e) 8 kg   (f) £1.60

C3 A Christmas cake weighs 800 grams. 75% of the cake is dried fruit.
What is the weight of fruit in the cake?

C4 Chloe is 180 cm tall. Her brother is 75% of Chloe's height.
How tall is Chloe's brother?

C5 There are 24 pupils in David's class. 75% of them can swim.

(a) How many pupils can swim?

(b) How many pupils cannot swim?

C6 A paddling pool holds 3000 litres when it is full.
How many litres of water are in the pool when it is 75% full?

C7 I think of a number. 25% of my number is 4.
What is 75% of my number?

C8 Find 75% of the number, if 25% of the number is

(a) 3   (b) 10   (c) 12   (d) 20   (e) 150   (f) 0.5

C9 If 50% of a number is 12, what is 75% of the number?

C10 Find 75% of the number, if 50% of the number is

(a) 18   (b) 24   (c) 100   (d) 10   (e) 120   (f) 1

*C11 My friends have eaten 75% of a cake. They have eaten 900 grams.
How much did the whole cake weigh?

D 10 per cent

How do you find 10%?

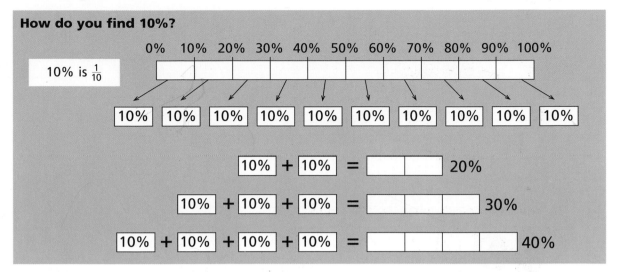

D1 Find 10% of

    (a) 30   (b) £70   (c) 120 cm   (d) 50 kg   (c) 700   (f) £150

D2 What is 10% of

    (a) £10   (b) £9   (c) £5   (d) 5 m   (e) £75   (f) 65 kg

D3 Find

    (a) 10% of 30   (b) 20% of 30   (c) 40% of 40   (d) 70% of 40

D4 Find 20% of

    (a) 30   (b) 70   (c) £20   (d) 80p   (e) 120   (f) 310 g

D5 Find 30% of

    (a) 40   (b) 60   (c) 110   (d) 90p   (e) £1   (f) 200 km

D6 Find 80% of

    (a) 20   (b) 30p   (c) £400   (d) 120 km   (e) £2.70

D7 A new car costs £15 000. I have to pay 20% deposit. How much is the deposit?

D8 Jan ate 10% of a trifle. Kate ate 60%!
Jan ate 75 grams. What weight did Kate eat?

D9 In Granny's will, Alice gets 10%, Beth gets 20%, Charlie gets 30% and Harry the rest.
Beth gets £240. How much do the others get?

D10 I have cycled 6 km and I am 20% of the way to home.
I have a rest when I am 70% of the way to home.
How far have I cycled when I stop for my rest?

E 5 per cent

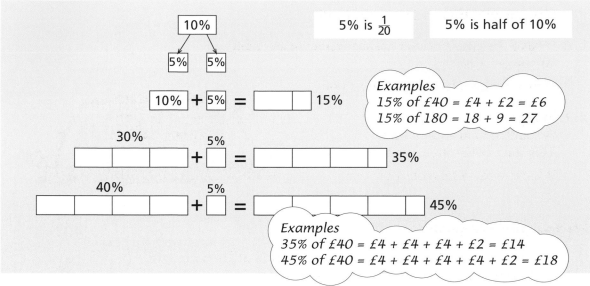

5% is $\frac{1}{20}$ | 5% is half of 10%

Examples
15% of £40 = £4 + £2 = £6
15% of 180 = 18 + 9 = 27

Examples
35% of £40 = £4 + £4 + £4 + £2 = £14
45% of £40 = £4 + £4 + £4 + £4 + £2 = £18

E1 Find 5% of

(a) 30 (b) £120 (c) £460 (d) 80 km (e) 500 g

E2 Find 15% of

(a) 20 (b) £140 (c) £320 (d) 90 km (e) £50

E3 Find 45% of

(a) 60 (b) £20 (c) £30 (d) 160 m (e) 2000 kg

E4 Find 65% of

(a) 80 (b) £120 (c) £260 (d) 50 g (e) £70

E5 Find 55% of

(a) £40 (b) £60 (c) £900 (d) 260 m (e) £10

E6 Find 95% of

(a) 20p (b) £60 (c) 50 g (d) £3000 (e) £5

E7 In his will Grandad leaves £50 000.
He leaves 20% to his son, 20% to his daughter,
and 15% to each of his four grandchildren.
How much money do they each get?

E8 There are 600 people at a concert.
55% bought their tickets from an agent.
The rest bought their tickets at the door.
How many bought their tickets at the door?

E9 There are 360 bottles of milk on a milk float.
When the milk float crashes into a wall, 65% of the milk bottles fall off the float.

How many bottles are left on the float?

E10 95% of the pupils in a school are present at assembly.
40 pupils are absent.

How many pupils belong to the school?

E11 Jon buys a car.
He pays 65% in a lump sum.
This leaves £420 still to pay.

What was the total cost of the car?

Fraction percentage puzzle

Match each of these percentages to its equivalent fraction.
Rearrange the letters to make the name of a fruit.

25%   50%   75%   10%

$\frac{1}{10}$	$\frac{1}{5}$	$\frac{1}{4}$	$\frac{1}{3}$	$\frac{1}{2}$	$\frac{3}{4}$	$\frac{2}{3}$
L	E	P	S	M	U	T

What progress have you made?

Statement	Evidence

I can find percentages of numbers.

1 What is
(a) 50% of £17   (b) 75% of 16 m

2 Find 10% of
(a) 630   (b) £130   (c) 75 g

3 Find
(a) 30% of 120   (b) 70% of £5

4 What is
(a) 15% of £80   (b) 65% of 120 m

I can write equivalent fractions
for percentages.

5 What fraction is equivalent to
(a) 50%   (b) 75%

10 Square deal

This work will help you
◆ simplify expressions
◆ use algebra to solve problems

A Hollow grids

To make a hollow grid
• choose a number for the top left square
• use the rules on the arrows to fill in the rest.

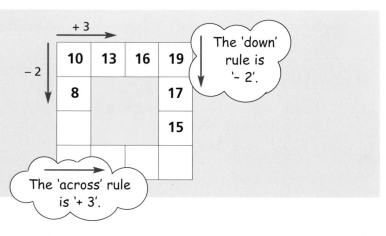

The 'down' rule is '– 2'.

The 'across' rule is '+ 3'.

A1 Copy and complete each hollow grid.

(a)
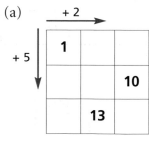

(b)
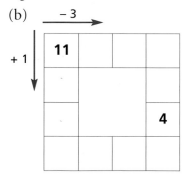

(c)
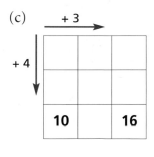

(d)
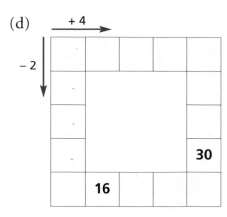

(e)
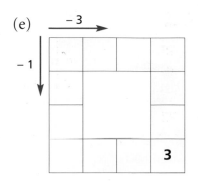

A2 For these hollow grids, find the missing rules and complete the grids.

(a)
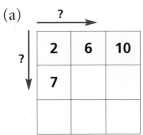

(b)
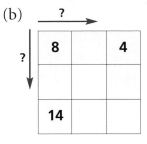

(c)

(d)
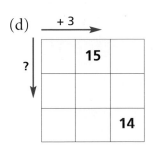

(e)
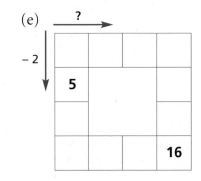

(f)
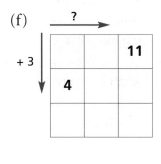

(g)

(h)
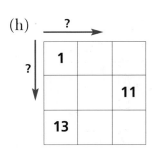

(i)
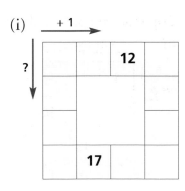

(j)
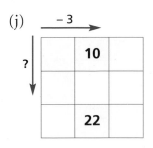

(k)
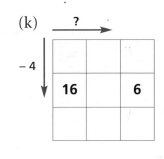

(l)
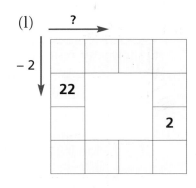

55

A3 These grids are all the same size and use the rules '+ 3' and '– 1'.

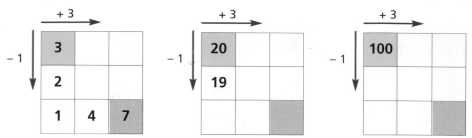

(a) Draw the complete grids.

(b) Copy and complete this table for these grids.

Top left number	Bottom right number
3	7
20	
100	

(c) Draw some of your own grids like this that use the rules '+ 3' and '– 1'.

(d) Put your results in the table.

(e) Describe a rule that links the top left number and the bottom right number for these grids.

(f) (i) Use your rule to find the number in the pink square for this grid.

(ii) Work out the number in the bottom right square when the number in the top left square is 130.

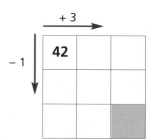

A4 (a) Copy the hollow grid on the right. Choose a number for the top left square and fill in the whole grid. Repeat for some different numbers in the top left square.

(b) Copy and complete the table to show your results.

(c) What is the rule that links the top left number and the bottom right number for these grids?

(d) What is the bottom right number when the top left number is 100?

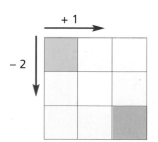

Top left number	Bottom right number

B Using algebra

You can use algebra to find rules for hollow grids.

For example, write *n* for the top left number and fill in the rest of the grid.

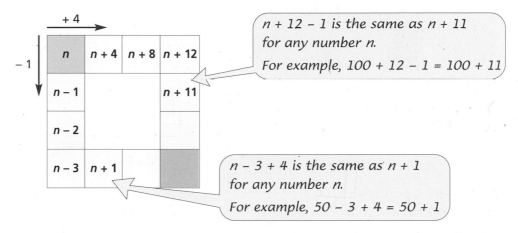

$n + 12 - 1$ is the same as $n + 11$ for any number *n*.
For example, $100 + 12 - 1 = 100 + 11$

$n - 3 + 4$ is the same as $n + 1$ for any number *n*.
For example, $50 - 3 + 4 = 50 + 1$

- Copy and complete this grid.
- Work out the number in the bottom right square when the number in the top left square is 190.
- What number in the top left square would give 100 in the bottom right square?
- Describe the rule to go from the number in the top left square to the number in the bottom right square.

This grid uses the rules '+ 1' and '– 5'.

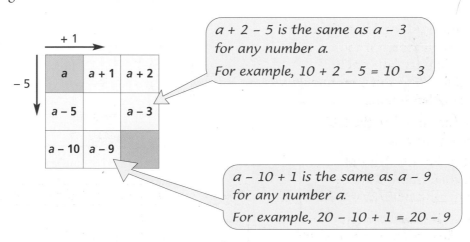

$a + 2 - 5$ is the same as $a - 3$ for any number *a*.
For example, $10 + 2 - 5 = 10 - 3$

$a - 10 + 1$ is the same as $a - 9$ for any number *a*.
For example, $20 - 10 + 1 = 20 - 9$

- What is the expression for the bottom right square?

B1 Copy and complete these grids.

(a)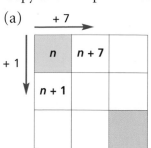

(b)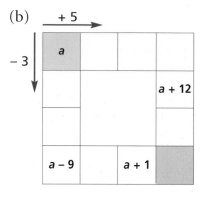

(c)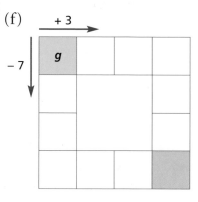

(d)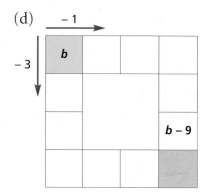

(e)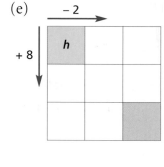

(f)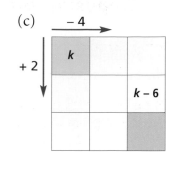

B2 For each grid in B1, work out the number in the bottom right square when the number in the top left square is 100.

B3 Write each of these in a simpler way.

(a) $f + 3 + 5 + 3$

(b) $y + 4 + 4 + 4$

(c) $x + 2 + 13$

(d) $z + 5 - 2$

(e) $p - 2 + 5$

(f) $m - 5 - 2$

(g) $q - 2 - 5$

(h) $w - 4 - 1$

(i) $h + 6 - 4 + 6$

(j) $a - 6 + 7 + 7$

(k) $b - 3 - 4 - 2$

(l) $c + 4 + 4 - 12$

(m) $d - 5 - 6 + 1$

(n) $e + 8 - 5 - 3$

(o) $g - 6 - 5 - 1$

****B4** Copy and complete these grids.

(a)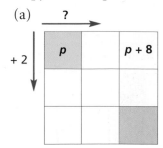

(b)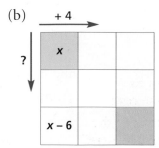

(c)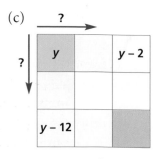

C Opposite corners

Investigation

The investigation is described in the teacher's guide.

Jo makes a set of hollow grids that use the rules '+ 4' and '– 1'.
She uses algebra to investigate adding opposite corners.

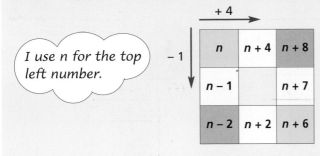

I use n for the top left number.

Adding opposite corners

Blue corners total: $n + n + 6$
                                $= 2n + 6$

Pink corners total: $n + 8 + n - 2$
                                 $= n + n + 8 - 2$
                                 $= 2n + 6$

The totals are **both** equivalent to $2n + 6$.
So I know that the totals will be equal no matter what n is.

C1 (a) Copy and complete this grid.

    (b) (i) What is the total of the numbers in the blue corners?

        (ii) What is the total of the numbers in the pink corners?

    (c) Are the totals equal?

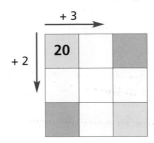

C2 (a) Copy and complete this grid.

    (b) Find the total of each pair of opposite corners.

    (c) Are the totals equal?

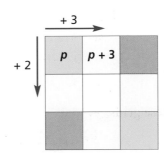

    (d) For this grid

        (i) What is the total of the numbers in the blue corners?

        (ii) What will be the total of the numbers in the pink corners?

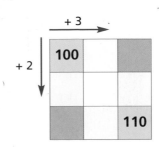

C3 Find four pairs of equivalent expressions.

A $n + 9 + n - 2$

B $n - 10 + n + 1$

C $n - 8 + n + 3$

D $n + 4 + 3 + n$

E $n - 8 - 3 + n$

F $n + n - 4 + 1$

G $n + 1 + n - 6$

H $n - 11 + n$

I $n - 7 + n - 2$

C4 Here are some more hollow grids.

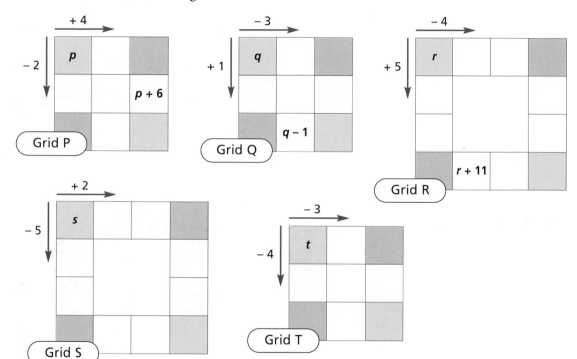

For each grid

(a) Copy and complete the grid.

(b) Find the total of each pair of opposite corners.

(c) Are these totals equal?

C5 Write each of these in a simpler way.

(a) $n + n + 3 + 7$

(b) $m + 6 + m - 1$

(c) $k + k + k + 5$

(d) $j - 3 + j + 5$

(e) $h + 1 + h - 6$

(f) $g + 1 + g + g + 3$

(g) $f + 5 + f + f - 1$

(h) $e - 3 - 6 + e$

(i) $d + 6 + d - 11$

(j) $c - 1 + c - 9$

(k) $b + 2 + b - 10$

(l) $a + a + 5 + a - 3 + a$

What progress have you made?

Statement

I can solve hollow grid problems.

Evidence

1 Copy and complete these grids.

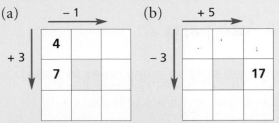

(a)

(b)

2 Work out the missing rules for these grids.

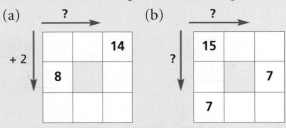

(a)

(b)

I can simplify expressions using addition and subtraction.

3 Copy and complete these grids.

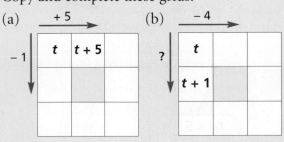

(a)

(b)

(c)

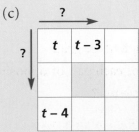

4 Write each of these in a simpler way.

(a) $k + 5 - 4$ (b) $j + 1 - 7$

(c) $h - 3 - 7$ (d) $g + g + 3 + 2$

(e) $f + 4 + f - 6$ (f) $e - 1 + e + e - 3$

(g) $d + d + d$ (h) $c + c + 1 + c - 2$

⑪ Pie charts

This work will help you to read information from pie charts.

A Into parts

There are only so many hours in a day!

How do you spend the 24 hours of a day?

Make a list of the main things you do on a school day.
Write down how many hours you do them for.
For example,

Sleeping	8 hours
At school	7 hours
....	

Only use whole hours and check that you have 24 hours altogether.

Use sheet 273 to draw a pie chart of your results.

On the second pie chart show how you spend a typical day at the weekend.

A1 There are 36 people in class 9P.
This pie chart shows their hair colour.

(a) How many pupils had blonde hair?

(b) How many pupils had red hair?

(c) What fraction of the class had

(i) brown hair   (ii) black hair

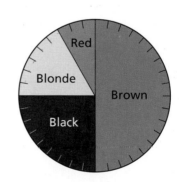

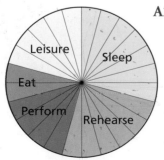

A2 This pie chart shows how a ballet dancer
spends his day.

(a) How many hours a day does he spend sleeping?

(b) He spends $\frac{4}{24}$ of his day performing.
What fraction of his day is spent rehearsing?

(c) What fraction of his day does he spend

(i) eating   (ii) on leisure

A3 A group of 20 pupils were asked what colour they thought should be used for a new school uniform.
The results are shown in this pie chart.

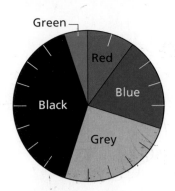

(a) Which colour had more votes, blue or grey?

(b) How many pupils chose blue?

(c) What fraction chose black?

(d) What fraction chose grey?

A4 In a class there are 36 pupils.
They were asked to name their favourite sport.
The results are shown in this chart.
14 people chose football,
6 chose tennis and 4 hockey.

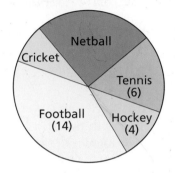

(a) (i) What fraction chose netball?

    (ii) How many people chose netball?

(b) Work out how many people chose cricket.

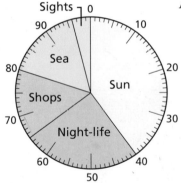

A5 In a survey 100 teenagers were asked what was the main reason they would choose a holiday destination. Their answers are shown in this pie chart.

(a) How many said the main reason was the sun?

(b) How many said the main reason was the night-life?

(c) How many said the main reason was the sea?

(d) What fraction said the shops were the main reason? Write this as a percentage.

A6 This pie chart shows what pets a group of children have.

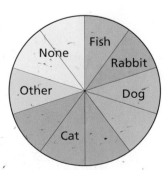

(a) (i) What fraction of the children owned a fish?

    (ii) What is this as a percentage?

(b) What fraction of the children owned a dog?

(c) What fraction owned a cat?

(d) 60 children took part in the survey.

    (i) How many of these children owned a fish?

    (ii) How many children owned a cat?

B Out of 10

'8 out of 10 cat owners said their cats preferred mice.'

Carry out some mini surveys on 10 people in your class.
Here are some ideas for topics

- What type of takeaway food do you like the most?
- Do you have a cat or a dog, or none or both?
- Do you come to school by car, bus, bike or walking?

Make sure there are no more than 5 choices people can
choose from.

Use sheet 274 to draw pie charts of your results.

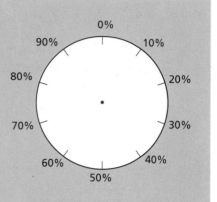

B1 In a mini survey 10 pupils were asked
what they had with their tea last night.
The results are shown in this pie chart.

(a) How many had chips?

(b) What percentage had pizza?

(c) What percentage had pasta?

(d) What percentage had either pasta
or rice?

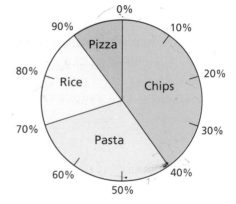

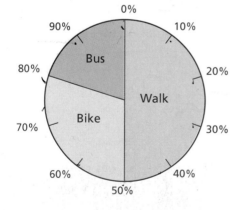

B2 In a mini survey 10 pupils were asked how they got
to school that day.
The results are shown in this pie chart.

(a) What percentage walked?

(b) How many walked?

(c) What percentage came by bus?

(d) What percentage did not come by bus?

B3 In a survey 20 people were asked what type of
TV programmes they liked to watch.

(a) What percentage said films?

(b) How many people said films?

(c) How many people said soaps?

(d) What percentage said news?

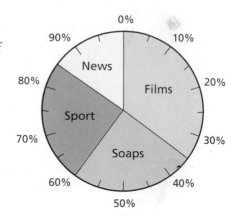

C Bigger surveys

Do they help at home?

A magazine surveyed 50 mothers of teenagers.

They were asked how much their children helped with housework.

This pie chart was drawn to show the results.

- What percentage said 'sometimes'? How many was this?

- What percentage said 'often'? How many was this?

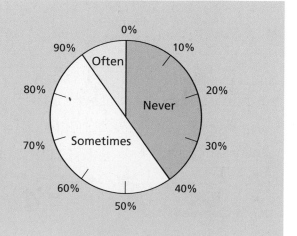

C1 In the same survey of 50 mothers they were asked who watched the most TV in their house.

Their answers are shown in this pie chart.

(a) What percentage said the parents watched the most TV?

(b) How many mothers was this?

(c) How many mothers said the children watched the most?

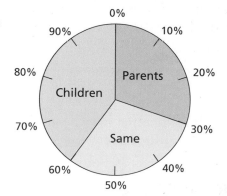

C2 A class of 30 pupils was asked what type of music they listened to most.

The results are shown in this pie chart.

(a) (i) What percentage of pupils said jazz?

(ii) How many pupils was this?

(b) How many pupils said classical?

(c) How many pupils said pop?

(d) How many said none?

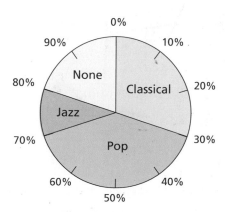

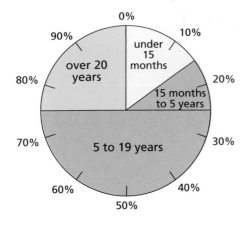

C3 This pie chart shows the ages of people in cases of measles in the USA in 1994.

(a) What percentage were aged under 15 months?

(b) What percentage were aged over 20 years?

(c) Around 1000 people caught measles in the USA in 1994.
Roughly how many were over 20?

(d) Roughly how many people between 5 and 19 years old had the measles in 1994?

Using a spreadsheet

You can draw your own pie charts very easily using a spreadsheet.

It makes no difference to a computer if the numbers are nasty!

Carry out a survey for your whole class.
Use the ideas at the start of section B if you want.

Then use a spreadsheet to draw a pie chart for the results of your survey.

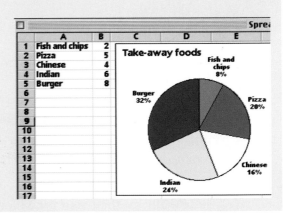

What progress have you made?

Statement

I can read information from pie charts.

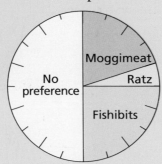

Evidence

1 The pie chart shows which cat food 20 owners said their cats preferred.

(a) How many said their cat preferred Moggimeat?

(b) What fraction said their cat preferred Fishibits?

(c) What percentage said their cats had no preference?

Probability experiments

This is about finding probabilities by doing experiments.
The work will help you

◆ estimate probabilities from the results of an experiment

◆ use estimates of probabilities

A The rope bridge

You will need a dice and a counter.

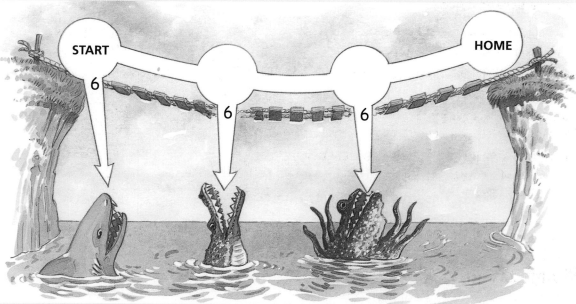

Put your counter on the 'start' circle.
Throw the dice.

- If you get a 6 you fall off the bridge and are eaten – end of game!

- If you get any other number you can move to the next circle.

Before you play, write down how likely you think
it is for a player to reach 'home' safely.

Play the game ten times.
Record your results in a tally table
like the one shown here.

Do these results agree with how likely
you thought it would be?

Result	Tally	Frequency
Safely across		
Fell off		
Total		10

Here are Andy's results.

The results show that he safely reached home 7 times out of 10.

We can say that he safely reached home $\frac{7}{10}$ of the time.

Result	Tally	Frequency
Safely across	卌 ||	7
Fell off	|||	3
	Total	10

The fraction $\frac{7}{10}$ is an **estimate** of the probability of safely reaching home.
We say 'estimate' because it may be slightly different for another set of ten games.

Look at your own results.
Use them to estimate the probability of safely reaching home.

Class activity

Show the results of your whole class as a dot plot.

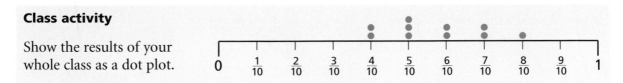

A1 Combine your own results with a neighbour's to give 20 results.
    Use these combined results to estimate the probability of safely reaching home.

A2 Here are the results from 5 pupils put together.
    They have not filled in the frequency column yet.

    Use the group's table of results to answer these.

    (a) How many times did they 'fall off'?
    (b) Estimate the probability of falling off.
    (c) Estimate the probability of getting home safely.

Result	Tally	Frequency
Safely across	卌 卌 卌 卌 卌 |||	
Fell off	卌 卌 卌 卌 ||	
	Total	50

A3 10 pupils put all their results together.
    There are 100 results all told.
    The frequency of falling off was 43.

    (a) What is their estimate of the probability of falling off?
    (b) What is their estimate of the probability of getting home safely?
    (c) Do you think these 'estimates' are better or worse than the estimates in A2?

A4 Using the estimate of the probability of falling off in question A3,
    roughly how many times would you fall off if you played the game

    (a) 200 times   (b) 500 times   (c) 1000 times

B Estimating probabilities

You need a coin and a counter

Home for tea?

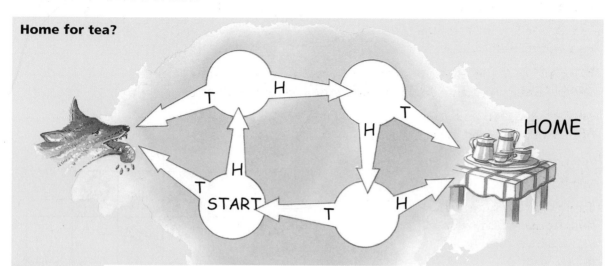

Rules of the game

- Put your counter on 'start'.
- Flip the coin.
- If it lands heads, move along the H arrow.
- If it lands tails, move along the T arrow.
- Keep going until you're eaten or safely home with a nice cup of tea!

Play the game 10 times altogether and record your results in a tally table.
Work out an estimate of the probability of getting home.

Show the results of your whole class as a dot plot.

Spend about 5 minutes on each of these experiments.

- Repeat the experiment 50 or 100 times.
- Use tally charts to record your results.
- Estimate the probability in each experiment.
- Say what you think would happen if you repeated the experiment a thousand times.

A bit dicey!

Throw two dice several times and record the results.

Estimate the probability of getting a 'double'.

T

Sunny side up

When you drop a spoon it can land

the right way up  or upside down

Estimate the probability of a spoon landing the right way up.

A moving experience

You need a dice and a counter

Make a larger copy of this grid.
Put your counter on 'start'.

Roll the dice and move
one square according
to these rules.

Stop when you hit a
win or lose square.

Estimate the probability of winning.

3 or 4
go up

1 or 2
go left

5 or 6
go right

The odd one out   a game for two people.

You need two dice for this experiment.

One person is 'odd', the other person 'even'.

Roll the two dice and find the difference between the two numbers.

- If the difference is odd the 'odd' person wins.
- If it is even then 'even' wins (count 0 as even).

Estimate the probability of 'even' winning.

How was your landing?

When you drop a multilink cube, there are three ways it can land.

Bobble up   Bobble down   Bobble at side

Write down what you think is the probability of landing each way.

Do an experiment to estimate the probability of landing each way.

Class 9J carried out a survey of cars passing the front of their school.
They noted whether they were red, black or some other colour.
Here are their results.

Colour	Tally	Frequency
Red	ЖЖ ЖЖ ЖЖ ЖЖ ЖЖ II	
Black	ЖЖ ЖЖ II	
Other	ЖЖ ЖЖ ЖЖ ЖЖ I	
	Total	

B1 What was the frequency of a car going past being

    (a) red   (b) black   (c) another colour

B2 How many cars did 9J survey altogether?

B3 Write down an estimate of the probability of a car going past being

    (a) red   (b) black   (c) another colour

B4 If 9J did a survey where they watched 600 cars passing,
how many roughly do you think would be

    (a) red   (b) black   (c) another colour

B5 Shena drops a cricket bat 50 times.
It lands front down on the ground 22 times.

    (a) How many times does it land front up?

    (b) Estimate the probability of the bat landing front up.

    (c) If she dropped it 1000 times, how many times would you expect it to land front up?

Ben runs a coconut shy at a fairground.
On Monday, he keeps a note of how many customers
win a prize and how many do not.

	Tally	Frequency
Wins prize	ЖЖ III	
Loses	ЖЖ ЖЖ ЖЖ II	

B6 (a) How many customers won prizes?

    (b) How many customers did not win a prize?

B7 How many customers did Ben have altogether on Monday?

B8 Estimate the probability of a customer winning a prize.

B9 On Tuesday, Ben had 100 customers.
About how many would you expect to win prizes?

B10 Ben charges £1.50 a go at his coconut shy.
How much money did he take on Tuesday?

*__B11__ Each prize costs Ben £3.50.

(a) How much would you expect Tuesday's prizes to cost Ben altogether?

(b) How much profit do you think Ben would make on Tuesday?

Just what I expected

You need a coin and a dice.

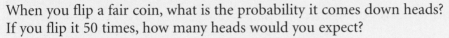

When you flip a fair coin, what is the probability it comes down heads?
If you flip it 50 times, how many heads would you expect?

Flip a coin 50 times and keep a record of the results.
Did you get exactly the number of heads you expected?

Compare your results with the other people in your class, using a dot plot.

Try a similar experiment to see how many sixes
you get when you roll a dice 36 times.

What progress have you made?

Statement	Evidence
I can estimate probabilities from games and experiments.	1 Karen drops a drawing pin 20 times. She notes whether it lands point up or down. Here are her results.

	Tally	Frequency
Point up	⊞⊞ ⊞⊞ ‖	
Point down	⊞⊞ ‖‖‖	

(a) (i) What was the frequency of 'point up'?

(ii) Estimate the probability of the pin landing point up.

I can use probabilities estimated from games and experiments.

(b) Donna drops the same pin 100 times. Roughly how many times would you expect the pin to land point up in Donna's experiment?

Review 2

Do not use a calculator for this review.

1 In a 'Pick an Egg' game at a school fete, some eggs are placed in sand.
Some of the eggs are whole, some are only half shells.
If you pick a whole egg you win a prize.

What is the probability of winning in each of these games?

(a) 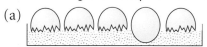   (b)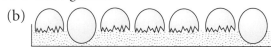

(c)    (d)

2 (a) 50% of the world's buffalo population is in India.
    There are 132 million buffaloes in the world.
    How many are in India?

  (b) Local councils are supposed to recycle 30% of their waste.
    One council collects 50 tonnes of waste each week.
    How many tonnes of waste should it recycle each week?

3 Copy these grids.
Work out the missing rules for each grid.
Use the rules to complete the grids.

(a) 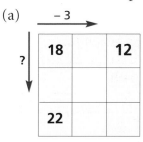   (b) 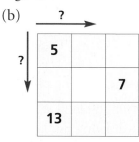   (c)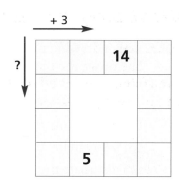

4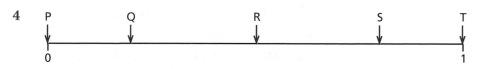

Which letter on the probability line stands for each of these probabilities?

(a) Getting a head when a fair coin is flipped

(b) Getting a 7 when an ordinary dice is rolled

(c) Choosing a red sweet at random from a bag of ten sweets, two of which are red

5 In a survey, 50 people were asked where they took their main holiday last year.

This pie chart shows the results.

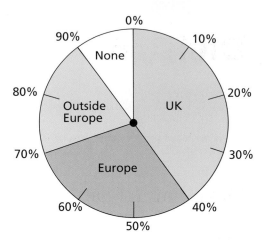

(a) What fraction of people in the survey took a holiday in the UK?

(b) What percentage of people took a holiday in Europe?

(c) What percentage of people took a holiday outside Europe?
How many of the 50 people was this?

6 Write each of these in a simpler way.

(a) $m + 4 - 2$ (b) $h + 3 + h + 5$ (c) $k - 5 - 7$

(d) $f + 7 + f - 4$ (e) $g - 3 + g + 7$ (f) $e - 5 + e + e + 7$

7 Jim sells T-shirts at concerts.
At one concert, 25% of all the fans there bought a T-shirt.
Jim sold 300 T-shirts at this concert.

(a) How many fans were at the concert altogether?

(b) 75% of all the fans had a copy of the group's latest CD.
How many fans had a copy of the latest CD?

(c) 15% of the fans were members of the official fan club.
How many fans was this?

8 Lauren is carrying out an experiment with a drawing pin.
She drops the pin and records whether it lands point up or point down.
This tally chart shows her results.

Landed	Tally	Frequency
Point up	HHT HHT HHT HHT HHT III	
Point down	HHT HHT HHT HHT II	

(a) How many times did she drop the drawing pin altogether?

(b) How many times did the drawing pin land point up?

(c) Estimate the probability of the drawing pin landing point up.

(d) What is your estimate of the probability of the drawing pin landing point down?

(e) If the drawing pin was dropped 200 times, roughly how many times would you expect the pin to land point down?

9 (a) Find the cost of four bags of garden compost costing £2.99 each.

(b) Find the cost of four bulbs at 49p each and a bowl at £3.50.

(c) A privet hedge is 50 cm high.
How long will it take to reach 2 m if it grows at a rate of 30 cm a year?

⑬ Division

This work will help you

◆ divide without using a calculator

◆ solve problems involving division without using a calculator

A The great divide

60 ÷ 5?

Split 60 into 5 equal parts.

Keep adding 5s until you reach 60.

What do you multiply by 5 to get 60?

How many 5s are in 60?

A1 Work these out.

(a) 18 ÷ 2 (b) 24 ÷ 3 (c) 36 ÷ 4 (d) 30 ÷ 5 (e) 27 ÷ 3

(f) 63 ÷ 7 (g) 72 ÷ 9 (h) 56 ÷ 8 (i) 66 ÷ 6 (j) 84 ÷ 12

(k) 28 ÷ 2 (l) 65 ÷ 5 (m) 52 ÷ 4 (n) 84 ÷ 6 (o) 105 ÷ 7

A2 (a) Do each calculation.
Use the code to change the results into letters.
Rearrange each group of letters to spell an animal.

D	B	F	G	H	I	K	M	P	S	A	L	R	E	Y	U	W	N	T	O
2	3	4	5	6	7	8	9	10	11	12	13	14	15	16	17	18	19	20	21

1 40 ÷ 20	2 38 ÷ 2	3 39 ÷ 3	4 42 ÷ 7	5 24 ÷ 6	6 120 ÷ 10
42 ÷ 3	45 ÷ 3	28 ÷ 2	63 ÷ 3	56 ÷ 4	70 ÷ 5
30 ÷ 2	42 ÷ 2	36 ÷ 3	57 ÷ 3	35 ÷ 5	25 ÷ 5
45 ÷ 9	81 ÷ 9	55 ÷ 5	56 ÷ 8	96 ÷ 8	49 ÷ 7
48 ÷ 4	32 ÷ 2	34 ÷ 2	26 ÷ 2	60 ÷ 4	78 ÷ 6
27 ÷ 9	32 ÷ 4	36 ÷ 2	22 ÷ 11	35 ÷ 7	84 ÷ 4
			90 ÷ 9	36 ÷ 9	52 ÷ 4

(b) Make up a set of divisions that give the word HAMSTER.

A3 Copy and complete these statements.

(a) $24 \div 8 = \ldots$ (b) $12 \div \ldots = 4$ (c) $\ldots \div 5 = 4$

(d) $32 \div \ldots = 8$ (e) $42 \div \ldots = 6$ (f) $\ldots \div 3 = 10$

A4 The six numbers in the loop fit into
the calculations below.
Each number is used only once.

Find the missing number in each calculation.

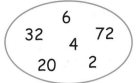

(a) $18 \div \blacksquare = 9$ (b) $28 \div \blacksquare = 7$ (c) $36 \div \blacksquare = 6$

(d) $\blacksquare \div 10 = 2$ (e) $\blacksquare \div 8 = 4$ (f) $\blacksquare \div 9 = 8$

A5 Find the missing number in each calculation.

(a) $50 \div \blacksquare = 10$ (b) $24 \div \blacksquare = 4$ (c) $64 \div \blacksquare = 8$

(d) $\blacksquare \div 3 = 6$ (e) $\blacksquare \div 5 = 8$ (f) $\blacksquare \div 9 = 6$

A6 Find the answer to each of these problems.
Write down the division you do each time.

(a) A box holds 4 cakes.
How many boxes would be needed for 20 cakes?

(b) A case holds 6 compact discs.
How many cases would be needed for 42 compact discs?

(c) Jim has 64 cherries. He shares them equally on top of 4 cakes.
How many cherries are on each cake?

(d) Prakash has 96 postcards.
He puts them in a book, with 8 on each page.
How many pages does he use?

(e) 100 postcards are shared equally between 5 people.
How many does each person get?

(f) Three people share a bill of £27.
How much does each of them pay?

B Remainders

An organic farm puts eggs in
boxes of 6.

How many egg boxes can
they fill with 57 eggs?

8 hens can nest in one chicken run.

How many runs will they
need for 61 hens to nest in?

B1 Rose makes 72 sweets. She packs them in boxes of 5.

    (a) How many boxes does she fill?   (b) How many sweets are left over?

B2 Gerry shares 75 marbles equally between his 8 grandchildren.

    (a) How many marbles do they each get?   (b) How many are left over?

B3 The answer to 23 ÷ 5 can be written '4 remainder 3'.
Do these in the same way.

    (a) 49 ÷ 5   (b) 69 ÷ 7   (c) 100 ÷ 9   (d) 55 ÷ 4   (e) 40 ÷ 3

    (f) 57 ÷ 2   (g) 57 ÷ 6   (h) 78 ÷ 5   (i) 83 ÷ 8   (j) 83 ÷ 4

B4 A taxi holds 4 people.
How many taxis would be needed for 30 people?

B5 How many 5-a-side football teams can be made from 62 players?

B6 How many of these car transporters
will be needed to transport 60 cars?

B7 Boxes 9 cm wide need to be stored on a shelf that is 80 cm long.
How many boxes fit along the shelf?

B8 Minh can carry 5 packs of paper at once.
How many trips would he need to make to move 64 packs of paper?

C Different ways

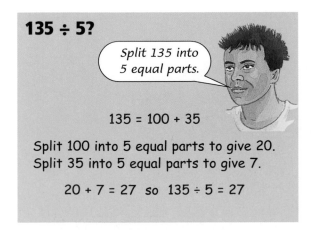

135 ÷ 5?

Split 135 into 5 equal parts.

135 = 100 + 35

Split 100 into 5 equal parts to give 20.
Split 35 into 5 equal parts to give 7.

20 + 7 = 27 so 135 ÷ 5 = 27

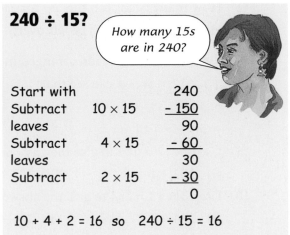

240 ÷ 15?

How many 15s are in 240?

Start with		240
Subtract	10 × 15	− 150
leaves		90
Subtract	4 × 15	− 60
leaves		30
Subtract	2 × 15	− 30
		0

10 + 4 + 2 = 16 so 240 ÷ 15 = 16

C1 Work these out, showing your method clearly each time.

(a) $125 \div 5$ (b) $112 \div 4$ (c) $180 \div 3$ (d) $156 \div 6$ (e) $252 \div 7$

(f) $180 \div 12$ (g) $225 \div 15$ (h) $375 \div 15$ (i) $156 \div 13$ (j) $252 \div 12$

C2 This pair of earrings has 4 turquoise stones.
Nina has a box of 132 turquoise stones.

How many pairs of these earrings can she make?

C3 Tony makes three identical pearl necklaces.
He uses 213 pearls altogether.

How many pearls are in each necklace?

C4 Nina has a bag of 192 red beads.
Each of these chokers uses 12 red beads.

How many of these chokers could she make?

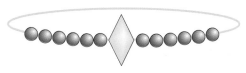

C5 Tony uses 108 grams of silver to make six identical bangles.
Find the weight of silver in each bangle.

C6 This pair of earrings is made from 8 grams of silver.
How many pairs could be made from 152 grams of silver?

C7 This choker uses 14 green beads.
Tony has a box of 100 green beads.

(a) How many of these chokers can he make?

(b) How many beads will be left over?

C8 Nina is making 5 identical necklaces.
She wants to use rose quartz beads and has a bag of 144 beads.

(a) How many beads can she use for each necklace?

(b) How many beads will be left over?

C9 This box contains 36 beads, arranged in 3 rows of 12 beads.

From $3 \times 12 = 36$, we can see that

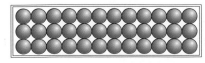

- $36 \div 12 = 3$
- $36 \div 3 = 12$

(a) Use $6 \times 17 = 102$ to give the answer to

    (i) $102 \div 6$ (ii) $102 \div 17$

(b) Use $13 \times 18 = 234$ to give the answer to

    (i) $234 \div 13$ (ii) $234 \div 18$

D Multiples of ten

140 ÷ 20?

How many 20s are in 140?

Keep adding 20s until you reach 140.

What do you multiply by 20 to get 140?

Start by finding how many 2s are in 14.

- How would you work out 80 ÷ 2?
- What about 420 ÷ 30?

D1 Work these out.

(a) 80 ÷ 2   (b) 80 ÷ 20   (c) 800 ÷ 2   (d) 800 ÷ 20

(e) 60 ÷ 3   (f) 600 ÷ 3   (g) 60 ÷ 30   (h) 600 ÷ 30

D2 Work these out.

(a) 160 ÷ 20   (b) 800 ÷ 40   (c) 120 ÷ 30   (d) 900 ÷ 30

D3 Find four matching pairs of divisions that give the same answer.
Which is the odd one out?

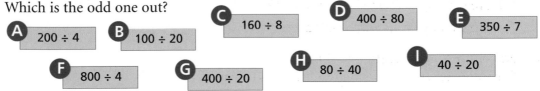

A 200 ÷ 4   **B** 100 ÷ 20   **C** 160 ÷ 8   **D** 400 ÷ 80   **E** 350 ÷ 7

F 800 ÷ 4   **G** 400 ÷ 20   **H** 80 ÷ 40   **I** 40 ÷ 20

D4 Work these out.

(a) 450 ÷ 50   (b) 300 ÷ 6   (c) 240 ÷ 80   (d) 420 ÷ 7

(e) 300 ÷ 20   (f) 480 ÷ 40   (g) 700 ÷ 50   (h) 390 ÷ 30

D5 Fiona packs 250 paper cups in packs of 20.

(a) How many packs does she make?   (b) How many cups are left over?

D6 Gordon puts 860 plastic knives in packs of 40.

(a) How many packs does he make?   (b) How many knives are left over?

D7 Find the remainders for these.

(a) 410 ÷ 20   (b) 200 ÷ 30   (c) 300 ÷ 40   (d) 300 ÷ 90

(e) 820 ÷ 50   (f) 200 ÷ 60   (g) 250 ÷ 80   (h) 570 ÷ 40

E Further divisions

How would you solve these problems?

A choker uses 21 blue beads.
How many of these chokers could
you make from 378 beads?

28 people win £336 in a lottery.
They share the money equally.

How much money does each
person win?

E1 Work these out.

   (a) 247 ÷ 13   (b) 375 ÷ 15   (c) 384 ÷ 24   (d) 665 ÷ 35

E2 The world's largest cabbage weighed 124 pounds.
If it was shared equally between 31 people, how much cabbage would
each person get?

E3 One of the largest beetroots ever grown weighed 464 ounces.
There are 16 ounces in a pound.
How many pounds did the beetroot weigh?

E4 The world's largest pumpkin weighed 495 kg.
If it was cut into 15 kg pieces, how many
pieces would there be?

E5 The largest marrow weighed 135 pounds.
If it was shared equally between 45 people, how much marrow would
each person get?

E6 The biggest salami on record weighed 676 kg.
If this salami was cut into 52 equal pieces, how heavy would each piece be?

E7 In 1997, a large Chinese dumpling was made to celebrate the return of
Hong Kong to China. It weighed 480 kg.

   If it was divided equally between 32 people, how much dumpling
would each person get?

E8 In 1989, a cheddar cheese that weighed 544 kg was made in Somerset.
If it was cut into 16 kg pieces, how many pieces would there be?

E9 A crate holds 18 bottles.

   (a) How many crates can be filled from 263 bottles?

   (b) How many bottles are left over?

E10 Daffodils are packed in bunches of 15.

    (a) How many bunches can be made from 400 daffodils?

    (b) How many daffodils will be left over?

E11 Jay puts paper napkins in packs of 24.
How many packs can she make from 550 napkins?

E12 300 people go on a school trip.
Each bus can carry 36 people.
How many buses are needed?

E13 (a) Copy and complete this pattern of divisions.

$$333 \div 9 = \ldots$$
$$444 \div 12 = \ldots$$
$$555 \div 15 = \ldots$$
$$\ldots \div \ldots = \ldots$$

    (b) Extend the pattern for another few lines.
What do you notice?

F Dividing decimals

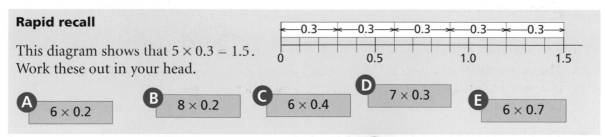

Rapid recall

This diagram shows that $5 \times 0.3 = 1.5$.
Work these out in your head.

A 6×0.2

B 8×0.2

C 6×0.4

D 7×0.3

E 6×0.7

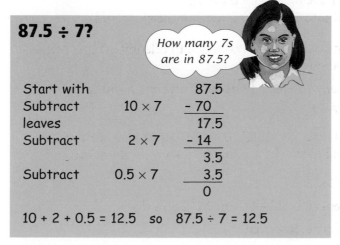

87.5 ÷ 7?

How many 7s are in 87.5?

Start with		87.5
Subtract	10×7	$- 70$
leaves		17.5
Subtract	2×7	$- 14$
		3.5
Subtract	0.5×7	3.5
		0

$10 + 2 + 0.5 = 12.5$ so $87.5 \div 7 = 12.5$

F1 Work these out.

(a) $48.5 \div 5$ (b) $86.4 \div 4$ (c) $67.5 \div 5$ (d) $54.4 \div 4$

(e) $97.2 \div 6$ (f) $113.6 \div 8$ (g) $93.1 \div 7$ (h) $130.4 \div 8$

F2 Work these out.

(a) $53.6 \div 8$ (b) $161.7 \div 7$ (c) $176.5 \div 5$ (d) $250.8 \div 6$

F3 Five friends go fruit picking. They pick 81.5 kg of strawberries between them.
They decide to share them out equally.
How much will each one get?

F4 A steel tower has six equal sections on top of each other.
The total height of the tower is 20.4 m.

How high is each section?

F5 The total weight of eight rescued seal pups was 123.2 kg.
What was the mean weight of the rescued pups?

What progress have you made?

Statement	Evidence
I can divide two-digit numbers without a calculator.	**1** Work these out. (a) $54 \div 6$ (b) $72 \div 6$ (c) $96 \div 12$ **2** How many 5-a-side football teams can be made from 37 players?
I can divide by multiples of 10.	**3** Work these out. (a) $120 \div 40$ (b) $600 \div 20$ (c) $360 \div 90$
I can divide three-digit numbers without a calculator.	**4** Work these out. (a) $124 \div 4$ (b) $108 \div 9$ (c) $143 \div 13$ (d) $117 \div 5$ (e) $360 \div 15$ (f) $210 \div 12$ (g) $800 \div 32$ (h) $380 \div 21$
I can divide simple decimals by a whole number without a calculator.	**5** Work these out. (a) $80.4 \div 6$ (b) $115.5 \div 7$ (c) $116.5 \div 5$

⑭ Bottles

This work will help you with your arithmetic.

⑮ Transformations

This work will help you

◆ reflect shapes and describe reflections

◆ rotate shapes and describe rotations

◆ translate shapes and describe translations

A Reflections

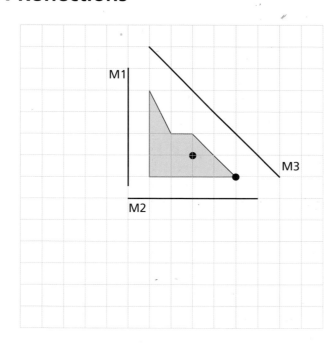

Micky can be reflected in any of the mirror lines shown.

Use sheet 275 to show where Micky will be when he is reflected in mirrors M1, M2 and M3.

Try reflecting Micky using:

● tracing paper

● the grid squares

This is how to use a piece of tracing paper:

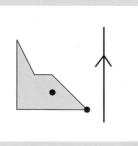

Draw an arrow on the mirror line.

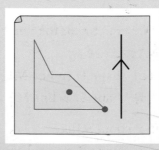

Trace the shape, mirror line and arrow.

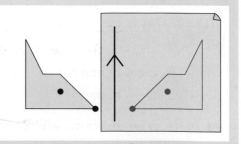

Turn the tracing paper over and carefully match the mirror lines. The arrow will help you position the mirror line at the right level.

When a mirror line cuts through a shape …   … it is reflected on both sides of the line.

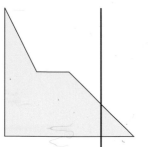 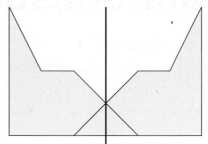

A1 This question is on sheet 276.

A2

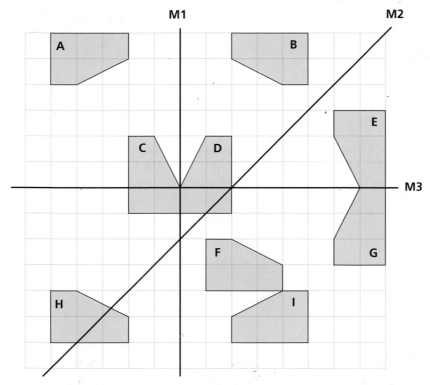

In the diagram above, B is the mirror image of A in the line M1.

Which shape is the mirror image after reflecting

(a) shape A in line M3   (b) shape H in line M1

(c) shape E in line M3   (d) shape C in line M2

A3 In the diagram above, what mirror line would reflect

(a) shape C on to shape D   (b) shape B on to shape I

(c) shape F on to shape C   (d) shape B on to shape E

B Rotations

On sheet 277, show where this shape
will be after a half turn with centre A.
(A half turn is a **rotation of 180°**.)

The point used as the centre is called the
centre of rotation.

Repeat this with point B as centre of
rotation, and then with C and then D.

- How did you make sure you
  turned it through a half turn?

- Does it matter whether you turn it
  clockwise or anticlockwise?

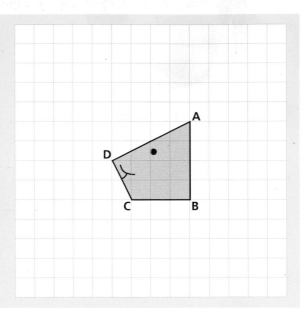

B1 This question is on sheet 278.

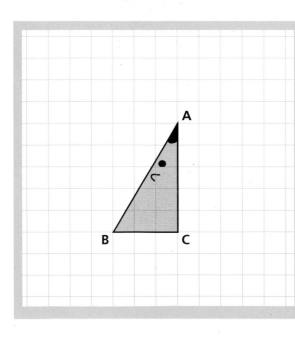

A quarter turn, or rotation of 90°, can be either

- clockwise (c/w) or

- anticlockwise (a/c)

Use sheet 279 to show where the shape will be
after a quarter turn with each of its corners as a
centre of rotation.
Do this both clockwise and anticlockwise at
each corner.

Label each new shape, for example

Rotation 90° c/w about A

How did you make sure that you turned
through exactly 90°?

Can you use the grid to help you?

B2 This question is on sheet 280.

B3 Each of the diagrams below shows a rotation of this trapezium.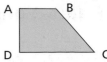
Describe each rotation by giving the angle and centre of rotation.

(a)

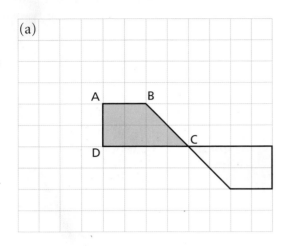

(b)

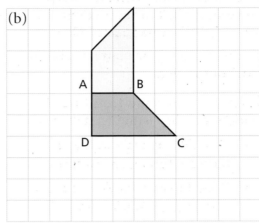

(c)

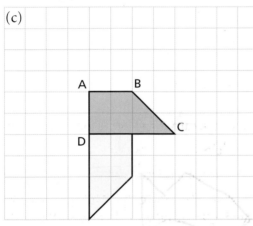

(d)

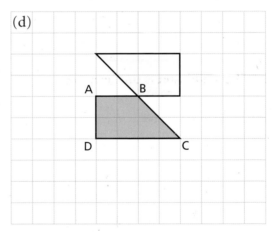

B4 On squared paper, draw the trapezium ABCD shown above.
Show its position after a rotation of 180° about D.

B5 On separate diagrams, draw ABCD and its position after

(a) a rotation of 90° clockwise about C

(b) a rotation of 90° clockwise about A

(c) a rotation of 90° clockwise about B

87

C Translations

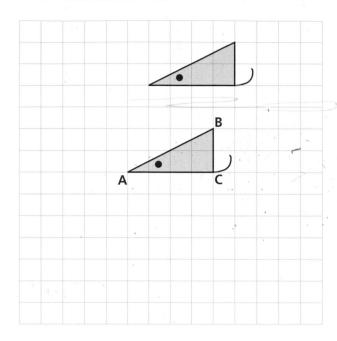

Millie has been moved up and across to the right. We say she has been **translated**.

- How far has point A moved across to the right?
  How far has A moved up?
- How far has B moved across and up?
- How far has C moved?

On sheet 281, complete each translation of Millie. Label each one.

C1 Look at this shoal of fish.

Describe accurately the translation that takes fish A on to fish B.

C2 Describe each of these translations accurately.

  (a) Fish A to fish D

  (b) Fish A to fish C

  (c) Fish D to fish E

  (d) Fish C to fish D

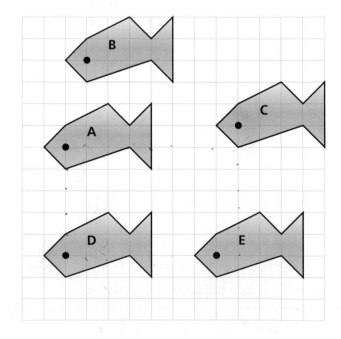

C3 This question is on sheet 282.

D Patterns

Patterns can be formed by transforming this shape on to the three other quarters of the square.

Here is the original and its position after a reflection in line M1.

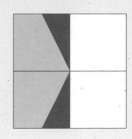

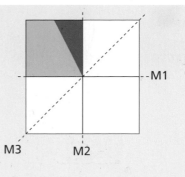

D1 Draw diagrams to show the original and its position after a reflection in

  (a) line M2   (b) line M3

The original shape can also be rotated.
Here is the original shape and its position after a 90° clockwise rotation about the centre of the square.

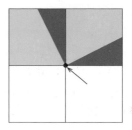

D2 Draw diagrams to show the original and its position after a rotation of

  (a) 180° about the centre   (b) 90° anticlockwise about the centre

Design your own patterns

Make your own design in a 2 cm by 2 cm square.
It must not have any symmetry and needs to be simple enough to make copies of.

Divide a 4 cm square into four quarters.
Make different patterns by transforming your design from the first quarter to the others.

Describe the transformations you used to make your patterns.

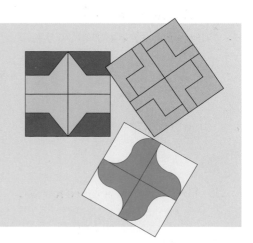

What progress have you made?

Statement

Evidence

I can reflect shapes in mirror lines.

1 Copy this diagram. Draw the position of the shape after reflection in the line

(a) M1   (b) M2

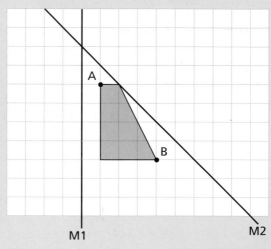

I can rotate shapes about points.

2 On the same diagram you drew for question 1, show the position of the shape above after a rotation of

(a) 180° about A

(b) 90° anticlockwise about B

I can translate shapes.

3 On the same diagram, show a translation of the shape 6 squares across and 1 square up.

I can describe transformations.

4 In the diagram below, describe the transformation which moves shape X on to

(a) shape A

(b) shape B

(c) shape C

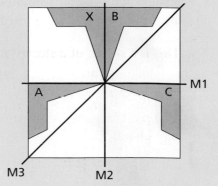

⑯ Groundwork

This work revises finding the areas of rectangles and shapes made from them.

The **area** of this rectangle is the number of centimetre squares it contains.

$$\text{Area} = 3 \times 4 = 12 \text{ cm}^2$$

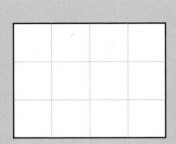

The **perimeter** of this rectangle is the distance all the way round it.

$$\text{Perimeter} = 3 + 4 + 3 + 4 = 14 \text{ cm}$$

1 For each of these rectangles
   - calculate the area
   - calculate the perimeter

(a)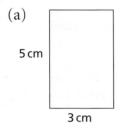
5 cm
3 cm

(b)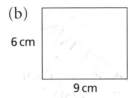
6 cm
9 cm

(c)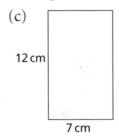
12 cm
7 cm

(d)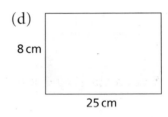
8 cm
25 cm

2 Find the area of each of these gardens.

(a)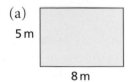
5 m
8 m

(b)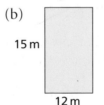
15 m
12 m

(c)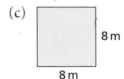
8 m
8 m

(d)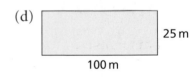
25 m
100 m

3 Each of the gardens in question 2 is to have a fence put around it.
   Find the length of fence needed for each garden.

4 This is a sketch of a storeroom in a school.

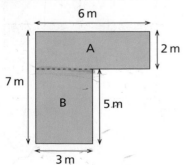
6 m
A
2 m
7 m
B
5 m
3 m

(a) Find the area of the rectangle marked A.

(b) Find the area of the rectangle B.

(c) What is the total area of the storeroom floor?

(d) Carpet costs £10 per m².
    How much would it cost to carpet this floor?

5 (a) Draw a sketch of this floor.
Fill in the two missing lengths.

(b) Show on your sketch how the floor
can be divided into two rectangles.

(c) Find the area of each of your two rectangles.

(d) Work out the total area of the floor.

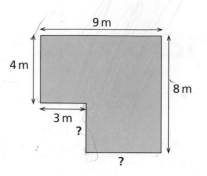

6 For each of these floors

• draw a sketch of the floor and add any missing lengths

• show how the floor can be divided into two rectangles

• find the area of each rectangle and the total area of the floor

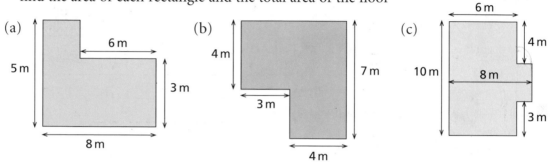

(a)

(b)

(c)

7 This room is having a new carpet laid.
Tape needs to be put around the edge to stop it fraying.

(a) What are the missing lengths x and y?

(b) What is the total perimeter of this room?

(c) Edging tape is supplied in 4 m rolls.
How many rolls of tape would you need
to buy for this carpet?

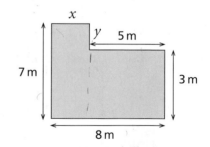

8 This garden is a lawn with a rectangular pond.

(a) Find the area of the whole garden.

(b) What is the area taken up by the pond?

(c) What area of the garden is lawn?

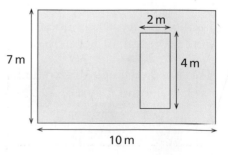

9 Find the area of lawn in these gardens.

(a)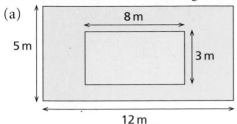

(b)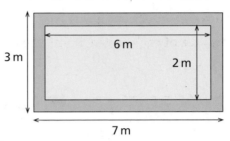

10 This lawn has a path around the edge. Find the area of the path.

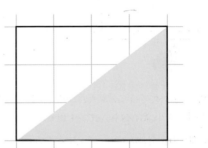

11 This yellow triangle has been drawn on centimetre squared paper. A rectangle has been drawn around it.

(a) What fraction of the rectangle is the triangle?

(b) Find the area of the rectangle.

(c) Find the area of the triangle.

12 Find the area of each of these triangles.

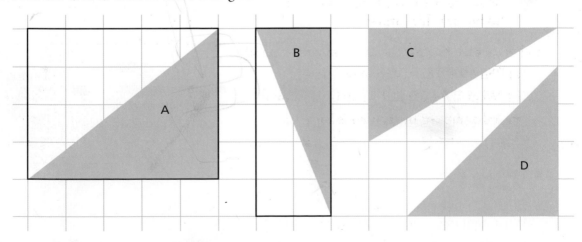

17 Number relationships

This work will help you

◆ revise multiples, factors and square numbers.

◆ find square roots

A Multiples

Multiples of 4 are numbers in the 4 times table.
Multiples of 5 are numbers in the 5 times table.

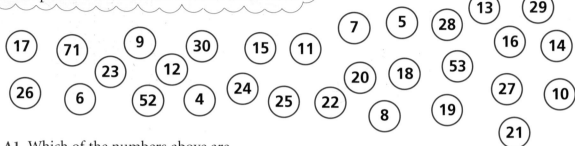

A1 Which of the numbers above are

(a) multiples of 4

(b) multiples of 3

(c) multiples of 5

(d) 1 more than a multiple of 5

(e) 2 more than a multiple of 3

A2 Here is a way of telling whether a number is a multiple of 3.

Is 1527 a multiple of 3?

Add together the digits   1 + 5 + 2 + 7 = 15.
Since the sum, 15, is a multiple of 3 then so is 1527.

Use this method to say which of these numbers are multiples of 3.

165   237   371   2652   3433   7632   26 571

A3 Sharon has some sweets.
She could share them equally between 3 people and have none left.
Or she could share them equally between 4 people and have none left.
Or she could share them equally between 5 people and still have none left.

How many sweets has Sharon got?

A4 1■1 is a multiple of 9. What digit does ■ stand for?

A5 All these numbers are multiples of 9.
What digit does each ■ stand for?

(a) 2■   (b) 5■   (c) 8■   (d) ■6   (e) 15■

(f) ■07   (g) ■04   (h) ■00   (i) 1■00

94

Patchwork patterns

Take some squared paper and number the squares in a spiral.
Go up to 100 at least.

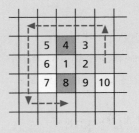

- Shade the multiples of 4 in one colour.

- Use another colour for numbers which are
  1 more than a multiple of 4,
  a third colour when they are 2 more,
  and a fourth colour when they are 3 more.

What happens if you use a different number (not 4)?

What happens with a different spiral?

B Factors

24 can be divided exactly by 4. We say 4 is a **factor** of 24.

Writing down all the possible multiplication pairs which give 24
uses all the factors of 24.

$1 \times 24 = 24$ $2 \times 12 = 24$ $3 \times 8 = 24$ $4 \times 6 = 24$

So the factors of 24 are 1, 2, 3, 4, 6, 8, 12 and 24.

B1 Which of these numbers are factors of 20?

4   5   6   2   40   8   10   1   3   20

B2 Write down all the multiplication pairs for each of these numbers.
Use the pairs to write down all the factors of each number.

(a) 21   (b) 18   (c) 48   (d) 30   (e) 16

B3 A **factor spider** can be used to show
all the factors of a number.

This is a factor spider for 24.

Draw factor spiders for these numbers.

(a) 20   (b) 18   (c) 36   (d) 42   (e) 23

W	A	N	D	S		M	I	G	H	T		H	A	V	E		C	A	U	G	H	T		I	N		S	E	A	W	E	E	D	?
28	13	6	40	56		8	26	21	7	49		16	34	10	27		17	52	4	9	88	38		47	2		23	95	37	46	14	18	11	

Copy the sentence and the numbers above on squared paper.
Cross out any letter which has below it a number which is

- a multiple of 3
- a multiple of 5
- a factor of 14
- a factor of 32
- a number with 11 as a factor

Write the sentence you are left with.

Multiples and factors bingo

Draw a bingo card with room for
ten numbers (or use squared paper).

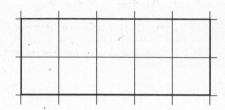

On your card write any ten numbers
from this list (no repeats):

4 6 7 10 12 15 16 18 20 21 24 27 29 30 31 33 35 36 39 40

Your teacher will tell you which numbers you can cross out using multiples and factors.

C Prime numbers

The sieve of Eratosthenes

You need some squared paper.

Write the numbers 1, 2, 3, 4, 5, … across your paper.

Write another 2 under the 2 in the top line.
Draw a line all the way across the
page underneath this.
This line is the 'sieve'.
Write any other multiples of 2 below
the line in the correct squares.
Carry on to the edge of the page.

1	2	3	4	5	6	7	8	9	10	11	12	13	14	15	16
	2														
			4		6		8		10		12		14		16

The next number after 2 which hasn't
yet been written is 3.
Write 3 above the line.
Now write the other multiples of 3
below the line in the correct squares.

1	2	3	4	5	6	7	8	9	10	11	12	13	14	15	16
	2	3													
			4		6		8	9	10		12		14	15	16

The next new number that hasn't yet been written is 5, so write 5 above the line and other
multiples below. Carry on like this until you can go no further.

Which numbers have not fallen through the sieve?

The numbers that have not fallen through the sieve are called **prime numbers**.
Prime numbers have no factors, other than 1 and themselves.

C1 Use your sieve to check which of these are prime numbers.

   37   19   27   51   33

C2 Work out which of these numbers are prime numbers.

   95   83   121   99   345

D Squares and square roots

When you multiply a number by itself you get a **square number**.

25 is a square number because $5 \times 5 = 25$. We write $5^2 = 25$.

Happy numbers

23 is 'happy' because

$$23$$
$$2^2 \qquad 3^2$$

$$4 + 9 = 13$$
$$\qquad\qquad 1^2 \qquad 3^2$$

$$1 + 9 = 10$$
$$\qquad\qquad 1^2 \qquad 0^2$$

If the number you end up with is 1,
the number you started with is happy.

$$1 + 0 = 1$$

If you reach another single-digit number,
the number you started with is sad.

$$42$$
$$4^2 \qquad 2^2$$

$$16 + 4 = 20$$
$$\qquad\qquad 2^2 \qquad 0^2$$

• Which numbers less than 50 are happy?

$$4 + 0 = 4$$

D1 Which of these are square numbers?

   36   50   49   100   99

D2 Copy the sentence and the numbers below.
Cross out any letter which has below it a square number.

D	O	G	S		N	O	T	I	C	E		C	H	I	L	D	R	E	N		L	O	O	K	I	N	G		A	T		T	R	E	A	S	U	R	E
35	10	25	49		12	60	8	9	16	81		4	26	45	36	70	64	24	1		100	36	16	4	40	15	9		50	25		44	56	32	36	81	16	49	72

Write the sentence you are left with.

D3 Copy this equation.

$$\Box + \Box + 6^2 + 7^2 = \Box + \Box + 5^2 + 8^2$$

Fit these numbers into the empty boxes
to make the equation true. 1^2 2^2 3^2 4^2

D4 What number is squared to make

(a) 9   (b) 64   (c) 25   (d) 49

4 is squared to make 16. 4 is called the **square root** of 16. We write $\sqrt{16} = 4$

D5 What is the square root of

(a) 36   (b) 4   (c) 81   (d) 100

D6 What are

(a) $\sqrt{64}$ (b) $\sqrt{1}$ (c) $\sqrt{9}$ (d) $\sqrt{49}$

D7 Use the $\sqrt{}$ key on your calculator to find

(a) $\sqrt{196}$ (b) $\sqrt{625}$ (c) $\sqrt{361}$ (d) $\sqrt{529}$

(e) $\sqrt{841}$ (f) $\sqrt{749}$ (g) $\sqrt{202}$ (h) $\sqrt{264}$

What progress have you made?

Statement

I can find multiples.

I can find factors.

I can spot square numbers.

I can find square roots.

Evidence

1 Write four multiples of 6.

2 Which of these numbers are multiples of 8?

40 28 36 72 76 56

3 Write all the factors of

(a) 48   (b) 30   (c) 36   (d) 100

4 Which of these numbers are square numbers?

24 64 36 54 20 25

5 What is

(a) $\sqrt{81}$ (b) $\sqrt{400}$

(c) $\sqrt{121}$ (d) $\sqrt{345}$

18 Simplifying

This work will help you

◆ simplify expressions
◆ use algebra to solve problems

A Perimeters

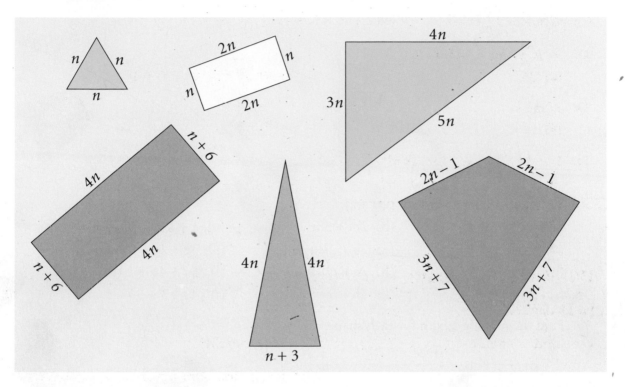

A1 (a) Find six pairs of equivalent expressions.

A $11p$

B $3p + 9 + p - 2$

C $3p + 6p + p$

D $8p + 2$

E $2p + p$

F $8p + 3p$

G $4p + 7$

H $p + p + p + p + p$

I $5p$

J $10p$

K $p + p + p$

L $3p + 1 + 5p + 1$

(b) Find the value of each expression when $p = 2$.

A2 For each of these

- find an expression for the perimeter of each shape
- find the perimeter of each shape when $m = 3$

(a)
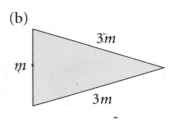

(b)

(c)
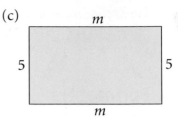

(d)
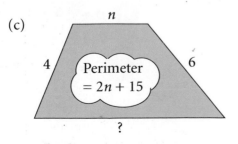

3m + 1

m m

3m + 1

(e)
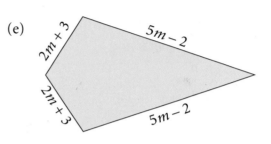

A3 Write each of these in a simpler way.

(a) $n + n + n + n$ (b) $2m + 5m$ (c) $k + k + k + k + k + k$

(d) $8m + m + 5 + 3$ (e) $7h + 2h + 3h$ (f) $5g + 2g + 8 - 1$

(g) $5j + 9 + 3j + 2$ (h) $5e + e + 9 - 7$ (i) $6d + 4d + 2 - 5$

(j) $6c + 3 + c - 2$ (k) $3b + 5 + 2b - 6$ (l) $4a - 3 + 5a - 1$

A4 Find the missing length for each shape.

(a)
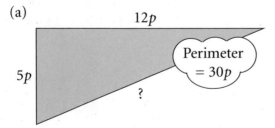

(b)
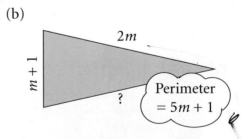

(c)
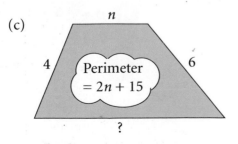

(d)
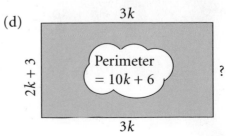

100

*A5 The perimeter of this shape is $3x + 2y$.

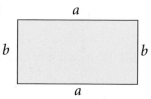

Find an expression for the perimeter
of each of these shapes.
Write each expression in a simpler way.

(a)

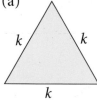

(b)

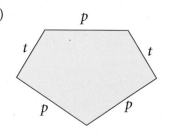

(c)

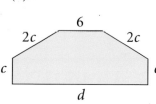

(d)

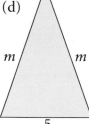

(e)

(f)

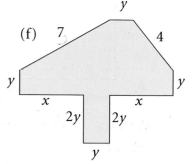

*A6 Write each of these in a simpler way.

(a) $x + x + y + y + y$

(b) $3m + 2m + n$

(c) $2p + 6p + 3q + 2q$

(d) $3g + 7h + 5g + h$

(e) $j + 3k + 6k + 1 + 9$

(f) $4x + 5y + 3x + 6 - 1$

(g) $m + 4n + m + 7n$

(h) $7 + p + 8q + 4p - 2$

(i) $6g + 7h + g + 9 + 3h$

(j) $7j + 8k + j - 10$

(k) $5a + 4b - 2 + 3b$

(l) $5c + 3d + 5c + 2d - 2 - 1$

B Missing lengths

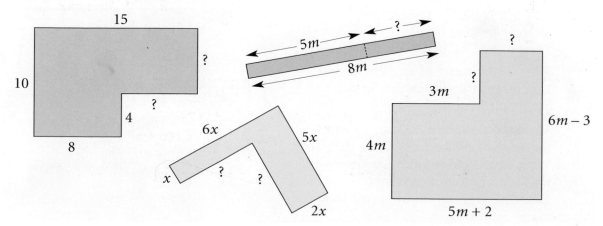

B1 Find four pairs of equivalent expressions.

A $m + m + m$ **B** $5m + 6 - 3m$ **C** $6m - 2m$

D $2m - 1$ **E** $3m + m$ **F** $4m - m$

G $m + 7 + m - 1$ **H** $7m - 5m - 1$

B2 Write each of these in a simpler way.

(a) $7p - p$ (b) $9m - 5m$ (c) $k + k + k - k$

(d) $9h - 3h + 5$ (e) $7h - 2h + 3h$ (f) $5g - 2g + 8 - 1$

(g) $5j + 9 - 3j + 2$ (h) $5e + 9 - e - 7$ (i) $6d + 2 - 4d - 5$

*****B3** Find an expression for each missing length.

(a)

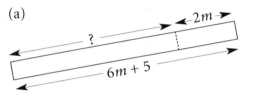

(b)

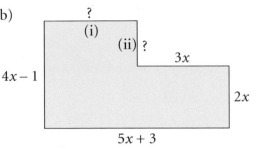

*****B4** Find the missing expression in each statement.

(a) $7n + \blacksquare = 10n$ (b) $14m - \blacksquare = 5m$ (c) $7k - 5 - 4k - \blacksquare = 3k - 8$

Missing piece

Each of these shapes is an 8 cm square
with a piece removed

- Find the missing lengths for each shape.
  What is the total perimeter of each shape?

- Find the perimeter of an 8 cm square
  with some other rectangles cut out.
  What do you notice?

- Write down expressions, using x and y,
  for the two missing sides in this diagram.
  Write down, and simplify, an expression
  for the perimeter of the shape.
  How does this explain what you noticed above?

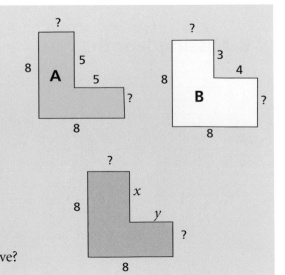

C Hollow magic squares

A hollow magic square is a hollow grid of numbers where the numbers in each row and each column add to give the same total.

The total for this hollow magic square is 24.

11	6	7
4		12
9	10	5

Totals
11 + 6 + 7 = 24
9 + 10 + 5 = 24
11 + 4 + 9 = 24
7 + 12 + 5 = 24

C1 Copy and complete these grids to make hollow magic squares.

(a)

	1	8
		7
4		3

(b)

3		7
5		
4	7	

(c)

1	8	13	
14			7
15	10	3	6

C2 Which of these are hollow magic squares?

(a)

5	1	13
11		4
3	14	2

(b)

5	3	1
4		6
0	8	2

(c)

2	10	1	3
8			6
4			3
2	5	6	4

(d)

10	8	7	5
12			1
6			13
2	9	8	11

(e)

3	9	13
10		7
12	8	5

C3 Some expressions are arranged in a hollow grid.

(a) Use $m = 1$ to make this a grid of numbers.

(b) Is your grid of numbers a hollow magic square?

(c) Jane adds the expressions in the top row.

$m+6$	$m+7$	$m+2$
$m+1$		$m+9$
$m+8$	$m+3$	$m+4$

$$m + 6 + m + 7 + m + 2 =$$

Copy and complete her working.

(d) Add the expressions in the bottom row in the same way.

(e) Now add the expressions in each column.

(f) Why do your results show that the grid is a hollow magic square with **any** value of m?

(g) Choose your own value for m and use the grid to make a hollow magic square.

C4 (a) Which of these are hollow magic squares?

A

$a+5$	$3a+6$	$2a+1$
$3a$		$a+8$
$2a+7$	$a+2$	$3a+3$

B

$4a+5$	$3a$	$8a+1$
$9a-2$		$a+6$
$2a+3$	$6a-1$	$7a+4$

C

$3+2a$	$8+3a$	$7-2a$
$10-3a$		$2+5a$
$5+4a$	$4-a$	9

(b) With $a = 2$, choose one of these grids to make a hollow magic square.

*C5 Which of these is a hollow magic square?

A

$7a+8b$	$2a+b$	$3a+6b$
$3b$		$8a+7b$
$5a+4b$	$6a+9b$	$a+5b$

B

$9p-2t$	$4p+3t$	$5p+2t$
$2p+5t$		$10p-3t$
$7p$	$8p-t$	$3p+4t$

What progress have you made?

Statement

I can simplify expressions using addition and subtraction.

Evidence

1 Write each of these in a simpler way.
   (a) $d + d + d$ (b) $2c + 5c$
   (c) $2k + k + 8k$ (d) $7h + 5 + h$
   (e) $9m + 4 + 2m - 2$ (f) $9n - 5n$
   (g) $6b - 3b + 5 - 1$ (h) $5a + 5 - a - 2$

2 Write an expression for the perimeter of each shape.

   (a) 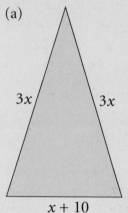   (b)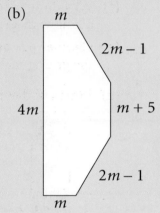

3 Is this a hollow magic square?
   Show all your working.

$b + 6$	$2b + 1$	$3b + 3$
$b + 5$		$2b - 2$
$4b - 1$	b	$b + 9$

*4 Write each of these in a simpler way.
   (a) $x + y + x + x + y$
   (b) $6m + 3m + 7n + n$
   (c) $5p + 6 + 2q + 1 + 2p + 9q$

⑲ Two-way tables

This is about data stored in tables.
The work will help you

◆ put data into two-way tables

◆ read information from two-way tables

A Making tables

Toadstools

Correctly identifying toadstools and mushrooms is very important.
Some toadstools are highly poisonous.
Sheet 283 shows some toadstools.

Some of these are spotty, some are plain.
Some have a collar on the stem, some do not.

Collar

Spotty with collar

Spotty without collar

Plain with collar

Plain without collar

Use a tally chart to find out how many toadstools are in each group.

- How many toadstools altogether were spotty?
  How many of these had a collar?

- How many toadstools had a collar altogether?

Copy this table.
Use your tally chart to fill in the
numbers for each type of toadstool.
These tables are called **two-way tables**.

	Spotty	Plain	Total
Collar			
No collar			
Total			

A1 Use your two-way table for the toadstools to answer these questions.

(a) How many toadstools were there altogether?

(b) How many toadstools were plain?

(c) What fraction of all the toadstools had a collar?

(d) What fraction of the spotty toadstools had a collar?

Egg grading

Sheet 284 shows some bantam eggs. Some of these are speckled, some are plain.
An egg longer than 4 cm is graded large, the rest are graded small.

- Measure each egg. Use tally marks to record data in a copy of this table.
- Use the tally chart to make a two-way table. Include the totals and check these.

	Small	Large
Plain		
Speckled		

A2 Use your two-way table from 'Egg grading' to answer these questions.

(a) How many of the eggs in total were

    (i) plain   (ii) speckled

(b) What fraction of the plain eggs were large?

(c) What fraction of the speckled eggs were large?

(d) Which eggs were more likely to be large, plain or speckled?

A3 Some students said what they saw when they looked at this picture.
Some saw a candlestick (C). Others saw two faces (F).

Boy (B) or girl (G)	B	B	G	B	G	G	G	B	B	G	B	G
Picture	C	C	F	C	C	F	F	C	C	C	C	F

This shows a girl who saw faces.

(a) How many girls saw a candlestick (C)?

(b) How many boys saw a candlestick?

(c) How many girls saw faces (F)?

(d) How many boys saw faces?

(e) Use your answers to copy and complete this two-way table.

	Girls	Boys	Total
Candlestick			
Faces			
Total			

A4 A class measured their heights in centimetres. Here are the results.

Boy/girl	B	G	G	B	G	G	G	B	G	B	B	B	G	B	G
Height (cm)	147	168	172	161	165	162	156	172	163	154	161	158	164	148	155

A researcher is interested in how many pupils are 160 cm or less tall.

(a) Use tally marks to record the data in a table like this.

(b) Write the results in a two-way table.

	Boys	Girls
160 cm or less		
Taller than 160 cm		

(c) What fraction of the boys are taller than 160 cm?

(d) What fraction of the girls are taller than 160 cm?

B Reading tables

Widow's peak

If you push back your hair, your hairline is
either straight or V-shaped.
A V-shaped hairline is called a 'widow's peak'.

This is a feature that is in your genes.

This two-way table shows the results from
a class survey.

What can you say about widow's peaks in this class?

	Boys	Girls
Straight hairline	8	10
Widow's peak	6	4

B1 Whether you can smell certain flowers or
not is thought to depend on your genes.

This table shows the results of a survey on
some adults with one such flower.

	Can smell	Cannot smell
Male	20	10
Female	18	6

(a) How many males took part in the survey?

(b) How many females took part in the survey?

(c) How many people altogether could smell the flower?

(d) What fraction of the men could smell the flower?

*B2 Do you think these results show that males or females
were more likely to be able to smell the flower?
Give your reasons.

B3 A gardener sows sweet-pea and
geranium seeds in his garden.

This table shows the colours of
the flowers that grew on each plant.

	Red	Blue	White
Sweet-pea	16	10	6
Geranium	18	0	12

(a) How many plants in total had red flowers?

(b) How many geraniums did the gardener grow?

(c) How many sweet-pea plants did he grow?

(d) What percentage of sweet-pea plants had red flowers?

(e) Which were more likely to have white flowers,
geraniums or sweet-peas?

B4 In class 9M there are 12 boys and 15 girls.
9 boys and 12 girls have brown eyes.
The others all have blue eyes.

(a) Use this information to copy and complete this table.

(b) How many pupils altogether had blue eyes?

(c) What fraction of the class had blue eyes?

	Boys	Girls	Total
Brown eyes			
Blue eyes			
Total			

B5 The local social services are interested in the ages of elderly people in a large home. A survey gives these results.

(a) How many of the elderly people were

(i) women   (ii) men

(b) What fraction of the women were 80 or over?

(c) What fraction of the men were 80 or over?

(d) Were men or women more likely to be 80 or over?

	Women	Men
Under 80	10	12
80 or over	14	6

C Experiments

Tongue tied

Scientists say that whether you can roll your tongue or not is inherited in your genes.

You can either do it or not – no amount of practice will make any difference.

Carry out a survey on two different groups, for example

- boys and girls in your class
- teachers and pupils

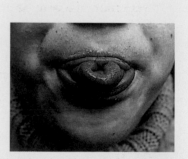

Record the data with ✓ for those who can, ✗ for those who can't.
Your data might look like this.

Boys: ✓ ✓ ✗ ✓ ✗ ✗ .....
Girls: ✗ ✗ ✓ ✓ ✓ ....

Put your data into a table like this.

Can you tell if boys are more able to roll their tongues than girls?

	Boys	Girls	Total
Can roll			
Can't roll			
Total			

...other genetic feature of humans is whether their earlobes are attached to the side of their head.

In a survey of a class the following results were collected:

Girls: ✓ X X ✓ X ✓ X ✓ X ✓ X ✓ ✓ X

Boys: X ✓ X X ✓ ✓ X X ✓ X X X ✓ X ✓

✓ stands for attached, X for unattached

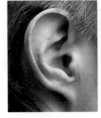 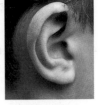

Attached   Unattached

(a) Copy and complete this table.

	Boys	Girls	Total
Attached			
Unattached			
Total			

(b) How many girls took part in the survey?

(c) How many girls had attached earlobes?

(d) What fraction of the girls had attached earlobes?

(e) In this class were boys or girls more likely to have earlobes attached?

What progress have you made?

Statement

I can record information in a two-way table.

I can read information from a table.

Evidence

1 A class did a survey on who wanted a school uniform. Here are their results (✓ means 'wants uniform').

Boys: X ✓ X X X ✓ X X ✓ X ✓ X X ✓ X

Girls: ✓ X ✓ ✓ X X ✓ X ✓ ✓ ✓ X ✓ ✓ X ✓

Use the data above to copy and complete this table.

	Boys	Girls
Want a uniform		
Don't want a uniform		

2 Here are the results from a survey on eye colour.

	Boys	Girls
Brown eyes	20	12
Blue eyes	5	3

(a) How many girls were in the survey?

(b) How many people took part altogether?

(c) What fraction of the girls had blue eyes?

(d) What fraction of the boys had brown eyes?

110

Review 3

Do not use a calculator for this review.

1 Work these out, showing your method clearly each time.

(a) 36 ÷ 6   (b) 72 ÷ 8   (c) 52 ÷ 4   (d) 51 ÷ 3

(e) 57 ÷ 5   (f) 46 ÷ 6   (g) 78 ÷ 9   (h) 53 ÷ 4

(i) 128 ÷ 4   (j) 132 ÷ 6   (k) 240 ÷ 30   (l) 350 ÷ 50

(m) 320 ÷ 8   (n) 270 ÷ 30   (o) 168 ÷ 12   (p) 322 ÷ 14

2 This diagram shows a trapezium ABCD and its image after a rotation.

(a) Describe the rotation by giving the angle and centre of rotation.

(b) Copy the trapezium ABCD and line M on to squared paper. Show the image of the trapezium after reflection in line M.

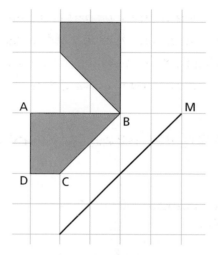

3 This is a picture of a lawn.

(a) Draw a sketch of this lawn and fill in the missing lengths.

(b) What is the total area of this lawn?

4 (a) What is the perimeter of this lawn?

(b) Lawn edging can be bought in 5 m rolls. How many rolls would you need to put edging along all the sides of this lawn?

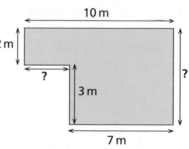

5 Copy the sentence and the numbers below on squared paper.

T	R	Y		H	I	S		S	T	I	C	K	S		P	L	E	A	S	E		R	O	Y
13	25	12		33	15	10		22	5	18	16	21	27		24	4	11	55	15	9		20	8	6

Cross out any letter which has below it a number which is

     • a square number   • a multiple of 4

     • a factor of 40   • a number which has 7 as a factor.

Write the sentence you are left with.

6 Work these out without a calculator.

(a) A youth group has 360 raffle tickets to sell.
They are shared out equally between the 15 members.
How many tickets does each member get?

(b) The youth group are also selling cakes. They make 250 cakes.
The cakes are stored in tins which hold 16 cakes.
How many tins are needed?

7 Find an expression for the perimeters of each of these shapes.
Write each expression in a simpler way.

(a)
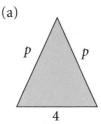

(b)
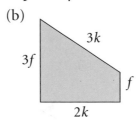

(c)
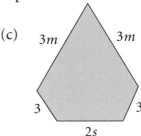

8 Justin carries out a small survey on whether
people are in favour of a school uniform.
He asks some pupils and some parents.

This table shows his results.

	Pupils	Parents
In favour	12	15
Not in favour	18	5

(a) How many parents did he ask?

(b) What fraction of the parents were in favour of school uniform?

(c) How many parents and pupils did he ask altogether?

(d) What percentage of all the people he asked were in favour of school uniform?

9 Write the total lengths of each of these strips as simply as possible.
Which two strips have the same length?

(a)
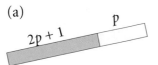

(b)
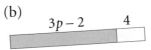

(c)
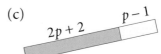

(d)
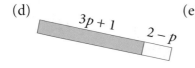

(e)
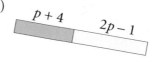

(f)
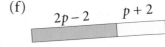

10 A 250 ml bottle of olive oil costs £1.25.
A 1 litre bottle of sunflower oil costs £3.47.

(a) How much would a bottle of olive oil and a bottle of sunflower oil cost altogether?

(b) How much would it cost to buy 1 litre of olive oil?

(c) How much more expensive is a litre of olive oil than a litre of sunflower oil?

Angles and lines

This will help you practise measuring angles and describing the type of angle.

You will

- ◆ learn about angles on a straight line and around a point
- ◆ learn about the angles inside a triangle
- ◆ revise how to draw a triangle given some lengths and angles
- ◆ learn how to construct nets for simple shapes

A Angles on lines

Are you being obtuse?

Draw an angle which is

- • acute   • obtuse   • reflex

Ask someone to check them for you.

> This is a cute little angle.

Estimating angles

Use only a ruler to try to draw each of these angles.

Now check each angle with an angle measurer. Keep a record of how good your estimates were in a table like this.

30°   60°   45°   90°
120°   210°   300°
180°   270°

Angle should be	My angle was
30°	27°

Angles on a straight line

Draw a straight line about 10 cm long.

Draw a second line from about the middle of the first.

Measure the two angles that are made.

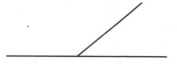

Angle 1   Angle 2

Repeat this with the second line at a different slope.
What do you notice about the two angles each time?

A1 For each of the angles in this diagram,

- say whether it is acute, obtuse or reflex and estimate the angle roughly
- check your estimate with an angle measurer

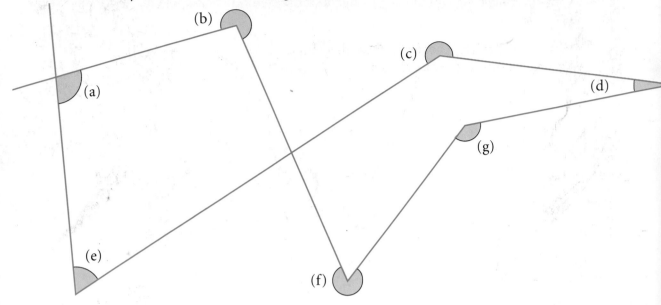

A2 (a) Measure each of the angles on these pieces.

(b) Which pairs of pieces make a straight line?

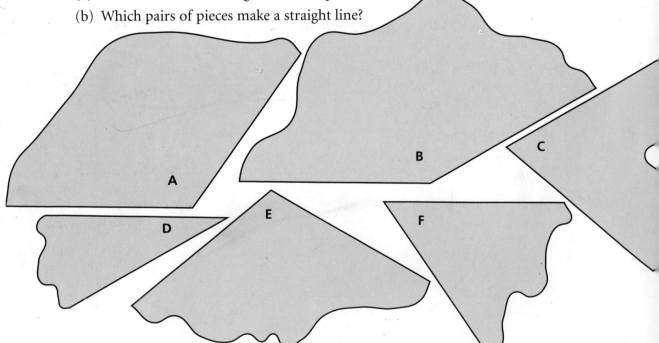

A3 (a) Could you make a straight line with two acute angles?

(b) Which of these pairs could make a straight line?

     acute + obtuse   obtuse + obtuse   right angle + right angle

Angles which meet to make a straight line
must add up to 180°.

Angle a + angle b = 180°

A4 Work out the missing angles in these diagrams.
Do not measure as the diagrams are not accurate.

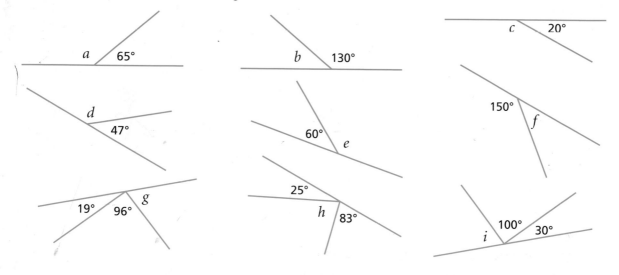

a   65°

d   47°

19°   96°   g

b   130°

60°   e

25°

h   83°

c   20°

150°   f

100°   30°

i

A5 Use the instructions below to make a full-size
copy of this pattern.

Draw it lightly in pencil first.

1 Draw a line 10 cm long.

10 cm

2 Measure an angle of 54°.

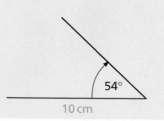

54°

10 cm

3 Measure 9 cm along the
new line.

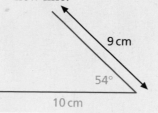

9 cm

54°

10 cm

4 Measure an angle of 45°
Draw a line 8 cm long.

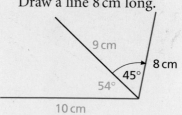

9 cm

8 cm

45°

54°

10 cm

Continue with   angle 36° then line 7 cm,
angle 27° then line 6 cm,
angle 18° then line 5 cm.

Join the ends of the lines to complete the pattern.

B Angles round a point

Fitting round a point

This square, equilateral triangle and regular
hexagon have sides with the same length.

What are the internal angles shown on each shape?

The picture below shows the triangle, two squares
and the hexagon around a dot.

What is the sum of all the angles around the dot?

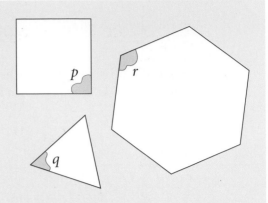

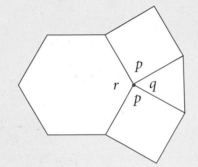

What other ways can you fit triangles, squares
and regular hexagons round a point without
gaps or overlapping?

Sheet 285 has several copies of these shapes.
Cut these out and investigate.

What is the sum of the angles round the point
each time?

B1 The cheeses below have had pieces cut out from them.
Which slice has been cut from which circle?

Check by adding the angles.

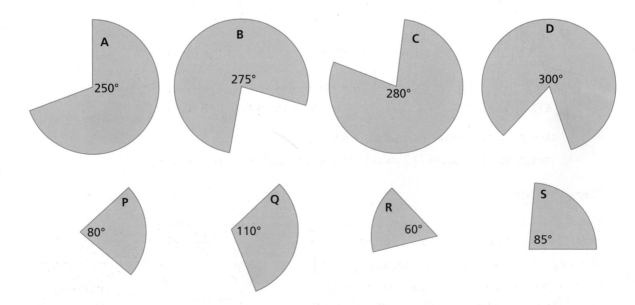

B2 Calculate the angles marked with letters in these diagrams.

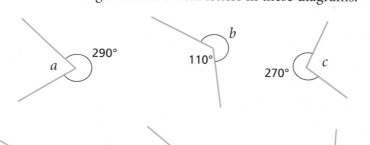

B3 In this circle a line was drawn from the centre to the top of the circle.
Two more lines were then drawn from the centre at angles of 120° from the previous line.

(a) Calculate angle *a*.

(b) If you joined up the three points on the edge of the circle, what special triangle would you get?

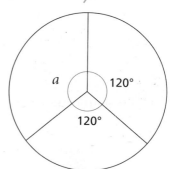

B4 What angle would you need to use inside a circle so that the points on the edge make a square?

B5 (a) What angle would you use inside a circle to give 5 points on the edge which joined to make a regular pentagon?

(b) Draw a circle of radius 8 cm.
Use an angle measurer to draw a regular pentagon in the circle.

B6 Use the method of drawing lines inside a circle to draw

(a) a regular hexagon (6 sides)   (b) a regular octagon (8 sides)

B7 What angle would you use inside a circle to draw

(a) a regular dodecagon (12 sides)   (b) a regular icosagon (20 sides)

Star patterns

The first of these patterns is drawn using a circle with 5 points equally spaced around the edge.

The second uses a circle with 9 equally spaced points.

Draw some patterns of your own using circles with different numbers of equally spaced points.

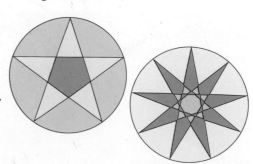

C Triangles

What happens when you put the
angles of a triangle together?

Does this work for all triangles?

What does this tell you about
the angles in a triangle?

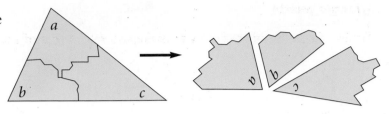

C1 Calculate the missing angles in these triangles.

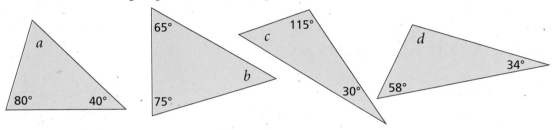

C2 These triangles are all right-angled triangles.
Calculate the missing angles.

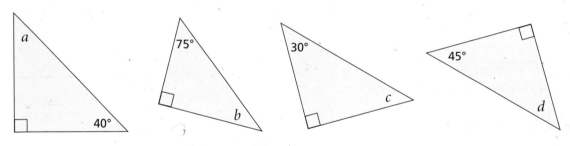

C3 These are all isosceles triangles.
Calculate the missing angles.

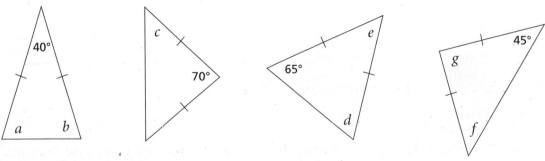

C4 What size are the internal angles of an equilateral triangle?
Explain how you worked this out.

D Drawing triangles

Triangle puzzle

Follow the instructions below to make accurate copies of these triangles on card.

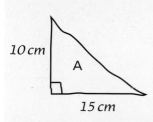

10 cm

A

15 cm

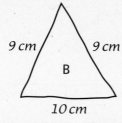

9 cm 9 cm

B

10 cm

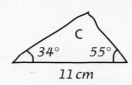

C

34° 55°

11 cm

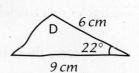

D 6 cm

22°

9 cm

Cut out your four triangles.
Can you put them together to make a rectangle?

To draw triangle B

Draw a base line 10 cm long.

Use compasses to draw an arc 9 cm from the left end.

Draw another 9 cm arc from the right end.

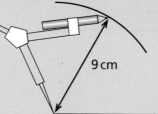

9 cm

10 cm

Where the arcs cross marks the top corner of the triangle.

To draw triangle C

Draw a base line 11 cm long.

Draw a line at an angle of 30° at the left-hand end.

Draw a line at an angle of 55° at the right-hand end.

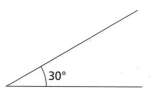

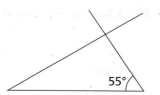

11 cm

30°

55°

Where the lines cross marks the top corner of the triangle.

To draw triangle D

Draw a base line 9 cm long.

Draw a line at an angle of 22° at the left-hand end.

Measure 6 cm along this line. This marks the top corner.

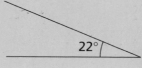

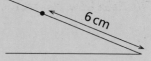

9 cm

22°

6 cm

D1 Make accurate drawings of the triangles in these sketches.
On your drawings, measure all the missing lengths and angles.
Add these to your diagrams.

(a)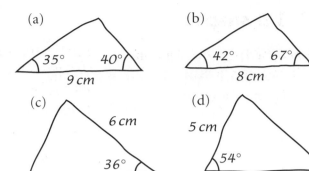
35° 40°
9 cm

(b)
42° 67°
8 cm

(c)
6 cm
36°
10 cm

(d)
5 cm
54°
8 cm

D2 (a) In this diagram angle $a = 55°$ and $b = 80°$. What is angle c?

(b) Make a full size copy of this drawing with $a = 55°$ and $b = 80°$.
Measure angle c to check the accuracy of your drawing.

(c) If in this diagram angle $a = 35°$ and $b = 110°$,
what would angle c be?
Draw an accurate diagram and check angle c.

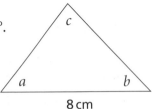

c
a b
8 cm

D3 This pattern has been drawn by drawing 6 triangles like those in D2 using the same base.

The angles in the triangles are

- $a = 15°$ and $b = 10°$
- $a = 30°$ and $b = 20°$
- $a = 45°$ and $b = 30°$
- $a = 60°$ and $b = 40°$
- $a = 75°$ and $b = 50°$
- $a = 90°$ and $b = 60°$

Draw the pattern.

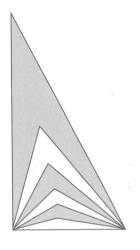

D4 Ahab's Sails have to make a sail for a large yacht.
This is a sketch of the sail.

(a) Make an accurate scale drawing of this sail using a scale where 1 cm represents 1 m.

(b) Use your drawing to find the length, in real life, of the third side of the sail.

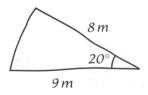

8 m
20°
9 m

D5 This is a sketch of a triangular-shaped field.

(a) Draw an accurate plan of this field using a scale where 1 cm represents 10 m.

(b) Use your diagram to find the length of fence that would be needed to go around the edge of this field.

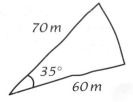

70 m
35°
60 m

120

E 3-D shapes

A **net** is a design that folds into a three-dimensional shape.

This is a net for a cube.

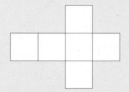

This is a net for a tetrahedron, a shape with four faces which are equilateral triangles.

To draw this net

- Draw an equilateral triangle with side lengths 5 cm.
- Draw other equilateral triangles on the sides of this to complete the net.

Octahedron

The shape in this picture can be made from two separate square-based pyramids.

Below are sketches of the nets for the pyramids. For each one start by drawing the square and then draw the triangles.

- Draw each net accurately.
- Put the squares on each of the shapes together to make the octahedron.

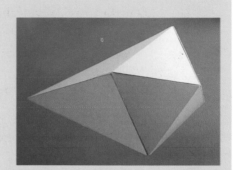

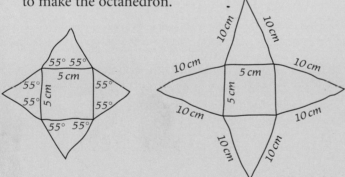

Cube puzzle

This net makes a right-angled pyramid with a square base.

Draw the net accurately.

Three of these pieces fit together to make a cube. Work with two other people to see if you can solve the puzzle.

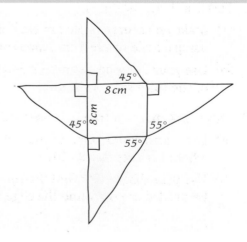

121

What progress have you made?

Statement

I can find missing angles on a straight line.

Evidence

1 Work out the missing angles in these diagrams.

I can find missing angles at a point.

2 Work out the missing angles in these diagrams.

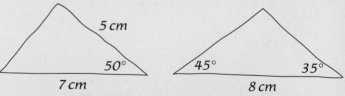

I can find missing angles in a triangle.

3 Work out the missing angles in these triangles.

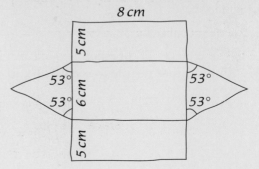

I can draw triangles given some of the side lengths and angles.

4 Make accurate copies of these triangles. Measure the missing lengths and angles and add these to your diagrams.

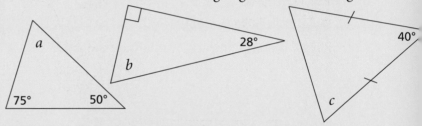

I can draw a net to make a solid shape accurately.

5 Draw this net for a triangular prism. Cut it out and check that it works.

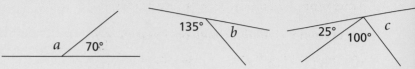

21 True or false?

For group and class discussion

Look at what each person below is saying.

Some things are always true, some are false.

For example: *All multiples of 5 end in a 5.*

The multiples of 5 are   5, 10, 15, 20, 25, 30…
So, for example, 10 is a multiple of 5 but it does not end in 5.
So 'All multiples of 5 end in a 5' is false.

For each person, say either that what they say is true,
or give an example that shows it is false.

Abby

*All multiples of 10
end in a 0.*

Beth

*To multiply a
number by 10,
just add a 0.*

*Don't forget!
'numbers' includes
fractions, decimals
and whole numbers.*

Callum

*A shape with
reflection symmetry always
has rotation symmetry.*

Dan

*If a triangle has two
angles the same size, then it
will have two sides the same
length.*

Eddie

*If you start with an even
number and add 1,
the answer is always a multiple
of 3.*

*If you start with an odd
number and add 3,
the answer will always be
a multiple of 2.*

Faith

Grace

*When you flip a coin 10
times you will always get
5 heads.*

22 Time and timetables

This work will help you

◆ use the 12-hour and 24-hour clock

◆ calculate with time (including using calendars and timetables)

A Using a calendar

January							February				
M	T	W	T	F	S	S	M	T	W	T	F
					1	2		1	2	3	
3	4	5	6	7	8	9	7	8	9		
10	11	12	13	14	15	16	14	15			
17	18	19	20	21	22						
24	25	6									

A1 Gerri's birthday is on 19 July.
What day of the week is this?

A2 (a) What is the date of the first Monday in March?

(b) What is the date of the last Saturday in August?

A3 How many Tuesdays are there in May?

A4 Fiona goes to the gym on February 4.
She goes again two weeks later.
On what date did she go to the gym the second time?

A5 Harry visits his cousin once a week on the same day.
He visits his cousin on November 27.
When is his next visit?

A6 Keme goes swimming on March 17.
He goes again four weeks later.
When did he go swimming the second time?

A7 Daisy goes on holiday on 26 August and returns on 15 September.
For how many weeks was she on holiday?

A8 Brooke starts a course of dance lessons.
She goes once a week for ten weeks.
Her first lesson is on 9 May.
When is her last lesson?

B The 12-hour clock

Use a.m. for a time after 12 midnight but before 12 noon.
Use p.m. for a time after 12 noon but before 12 midnight.

For example:
- Quarter past nine in the morning is 9:15 **a.m.**
- Quarter past nine in the evening is 9:15 **p.m.**

B1 Write the times in these sentences using a.m. or p.m.

(a) Rose eats her breakfast at ten past eight.

(b) Colin eats his lunch at half past one.

(c) Jamie gets up for school at quarter to eight.

(d) Nina goes to the library at twenty past eleven.

(e) Ken turns out the light and goes to sleep at twenty to eleven.

B2 This time line shows some things Liz does one day after school.

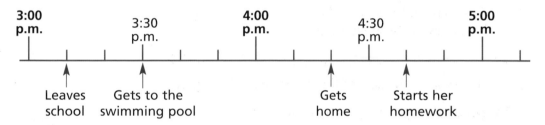

(a) What time does she leave school?

(b) How long does it take her to get from school to the swimming pool?

(c) She spends 45 minutes at the swimming pool and then walks home.

(i) When does she leave the swimming pool?

(ii) How long does it take her to walk home?

(d) She spends 1 hour and 20 minutes on her homework.
When does she finish it?

(e) How long is it between Liz leaving school and starting her homework?

B3 How long is it

(a) from 3:40 p.m. to 4:20 p.m.   (b) from 1:30 a.m. to 3 a.m.

(c) from 1:10 p.m. to 3:30 p.m.   (d) from 11:25 a.m. to 2:10 p.m.

B4 Sara wants to watch a film on TV. It starts at 7:35 p.m.
She finishes her tea at twenty past six.
How long does she have before the film starts?

C The 24-hour clock

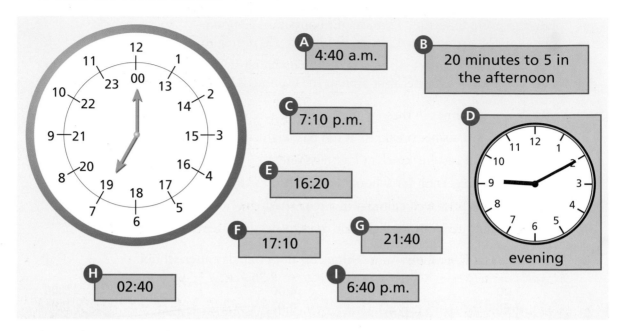

A 4:40 a.m.

B 20 minutes to 5 in the afternoon

C 7:10 p.m.

D evening

E 16:20

F 17:10

G 21:40

H 02:40

I 6:40 p.m.

C1 Four pairs of friends have arranged to meet.

Alice: My train arrives at 13:15. I'm meeting my friend then.

Bindoo: We're meeting at 9:40 a.m.

Carol: We're meeting at a quarter past 3 to go shopping.

Daisy: I'm meeting my friend at 1:15 p.m. to go for lunch together.

Ela: My bus arrives at 21:30 and we're meeting ten minutes later.

Francis: My bus leaves at 15:00 and I'm meeting my friend 15 minutes later.

Gayarri: We're meeting at twenty to 10 to go to a late night film.

Helga: I'm catching the 08:50 train and meeting my friend 50 minutes later.

(a) Who is Alice meeting?

(b) Match up the other pairs of friends.

C2 Copy and complete this table.

12-hour clock	24-hour clock
2:30 p.m.	14:30
5:15 p.m.	
	06:10
12:25 p.m.	
	21:50
4:35 a.m.	
6:25 p.m.	
	23:15
10:10 a.m.	
7:40 p.m.	

C3 Write these as 12-hour clock times using a.m. or p.m.

(a) 09:00   (b) 13:10   (c) 11:30   (d) 15:40   (e) 22:10

C4 Put these times in order, earliest first.

21:40   6:45 a.m.   1:00 p.m.   02:05   18:09   8:35 p.m.   16:00

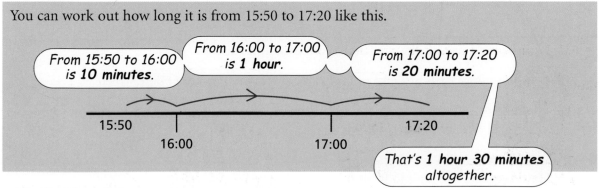

You can work out how long it is from 15:50 to 17:20 like this.

From 15:50 to 16:00 is **10 minutes**.

From 16:00 to 17:00 is **1 hour**.

From 17:00 to 17:20 is **20 minutes**.

15:50   16:00   17:00   17:20

That's **1 hour 30 minutes** altogether.

C5 How long is it

(a) from 06:45 to 07:15   (b) from 15:55 to 16:10

(c) from 09:25 to 10:40   (d) from 19:35 to 21:15

C6 Sasha wants to go to a film. It starts at 20:20.
She leaves home at 19:45.
How long has she got before the film starts?

C7 A film starts at 21:30 and finishes at 23:10. How long is it?

C8 Gill arrived at the railway station at five past three in the afternoon.
She got on the 15:32 train.
How long did she wait?

*C9 Solve the murder mystery 'Time to kill' on sheet 287.

D Timetables

Toneton Bus Services Route Q

Mondays to Saturdays (except Bank Holidays)

Newmill Park	0830	0845	0900	0915	09
Shepherd's Way	0835	0850	0905	0920	09
Galmington Street	0840	0855	0910	0925	09
High Street	0847	0902	0917	0932	09

Westexpress Train Services

Mondays to Fridays

Exborough depart	Toneton depart	London arrive
1043	1111	1321
1131	1200	1352
1236	—	1446
1336	1406	1605
1427	1456	1651
1531	—	1749
—	1525	1754

Use the bus timetable to answer questions D1 to D5.

D1 Jenny gets on the 8:30 a.m. bus at Newmill Park.
What time will she arrive at Galmington Street?

D2 Pete starts works at 9:30 a.m. in a High Street shop.
What is the latest bus he can catch from Newmill Park?

D3 How long does each bus take to go from Newmill Park to the High Street?

D4 Manjit gets on the bus at Shepherd's Way at ten to 9 in the morning.
When will she get to the High Street?

D5 Jan is at Newmill Park at 8:50 a.m.
How long will she have to wait for the next bus to Galmington Street?

Use the Westexpress train timetable to answer questions D6 to D10.

D6 When does the 1043 from Exborough arrive in London?

D7 Keith catches the 1336 train at Exborough and arrives in London on time.
How long was he on the train?

D8 Meena catches the 1525 train at Toneton.
How long will it take her to get to London?

D9 Gordon lives in Exborough and needs to be in London by 5 p.m.
What is the latest train he can catch?

D10 Sue needs to be in London for a 4 p.m. meeting.
What is the latest train she can catch from Toneton?

GREED EASTERN Train Services							Manningtree–Harwich	
Manningtree	1604	1711	1755	1838	1934	2030	2056	2212
Mistley	1608	1715	1759	1842	1938	2034	2101	2216
Wrabness	1613	1720	1804	1847	1943	2039	2106	2221
Harwich International	1620	1728	1812	1854	1951	2047	2113	2228
Dovercourt	1623	1731	1815	1857	1954	2050	2116	2231
Harwich Town	1625	1735	1819	1859	1956	2052	2118	2233

D11 You are at Manningtree at 5:30 p.m.
How long do you have to wait for a train to Harwich Town?

D12 You are at Wrabness at 6:00 p.m.
How long do you have to wait for a train to Dovercourt?

D13 Find the train which leaves Manningtree at 2056.
How long does it take to get to Harwich Town?

D14 Find the train which leaves Mistley at 1759.
How long does it take to get to Harwich International?

D15 You need to be at Dovercourt by 8:00 p.m.
What is the latest train you can catch from Manningtree?

D16 You are at Mistley and you need to be at Harwich International by 9 p.m.
What is the latest train you can catch?

D17 How many trains leave Wrabness for Harwich Town between
5 o'clock and 8 o'clock in the evening?

What progress have you made?

Statement	Evidence
I can use a calendar.	**1** If 4 July is a Wednesday, what day is 18 July?
I can use the 12-hour and 24-hour clock.	**2** (a) Write 3:20 p.m. as a 24-hour clock time. (b) Write 03:30 using a.m. or p.m.
I can use timetables.	**3** Use the above timetable. (a) How long does the 1755 train from Manningtree take to get to Harwich Town? (b) You are at Manningtree at 8 p.m. and you catch the first train to Mistley. When do you catch the train?

23 More negative numbers

This work will help you add negative numbers.

A Hot and cold

A1 (a) Which of these temperatures is lowest?

(b) Which temperature is highest?

−5°C ⁻10°C 0°C ⁻4°C

A2 The temperature outside my house at 6 p.m. was 2°C.
By midnight the temperature had dropped 7 degrees.
What was the temperature at midnight?

A3 The greatest change in temperature in Britain in a single day
happened in Tayside in 1978.
The temperature went up from ⁻7°C to 22°C.
By how many degrees did the temperature go up?

A4 In 1892 the temperature in Verkhoyansk, Siberia fell to ⁻70°C.
In Al'Aziziyah, Libya in 1922 the temperature rose to 58°C.
What is the difference between these unusual temperatures?

A5 For every 100 metres you go up, the air cools by about 1 degree.

One day the temperature at sea level on the Isle of Mull was 8°C.

(a) What was the temperature at the top of Bienn na Croise,
500 m above sea level, roughly?

(b) Roughly what was the temperature at the top of
Ben More, 1000 m above sea level?

(c) On the top of one mountain, the temperature was 4°C.
About how high do you think the mountain was?

(d) What height are you at, if the temperature is 7°C?

(e) What height are you at, if it is ⁻3°C?

B From temperature to number

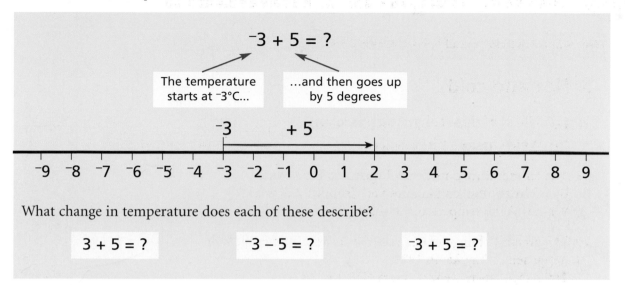

-3 + 5 = ?

The temperature starts at -3°C...   ...and then goes up by 5 degrees

-3   + 5

-9 -8 -7 -6 -5 -4 -3 -2 -1 0 1 2 3 4 5 6 7 8 9

What change in temperature does each of these describe?

$3 + 5 = ?$ $-3 - 5 = ?$ $-3 + 5 = ?$

B1 (a) Match each calculation to a change in temperature.

(b) Work out the answer to each calculation.

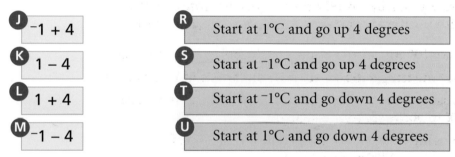

J -1 + 4   **R** Start at 1°C and go up 4 degrees

K 1 - 4   **S** Start at -1°C and go up 4 degrees

L 1 + 4   **T** Start at -1°C and go down 4 degrees

M -1 - 4   **U** Start at 1°C and go down 4 degrees

For these calculations you may find it useful to make a sketch of a number line.

B2 Copy and complete these.

(a) $-2 + 3 =$ (b) $-6 + 2 =$ (c) $-8 + 8 =$ (d) $-8 + 10 =$

(e) $-1 + 2 =$ (f) $-2 + 5 =$ (g) $-3 + 5 =$ (h) $-1 + 6 =$

B3 Copy and complete these.

(a) $3 - 2 =$ (b) $3 - 4 =$ (c) $-5 - 4 =$ (d) $-3 - 3 =$

(e) $0 - 4 =$ (f) $4 - 7 =$ (g) $-7 - 4 =$ (h) $-3 - 0 =$

B4 Copy and complete these.

(a) $-3 + 2 =$ (b) $-2 - 8 =$ (c) $-5 + 4 =$ (d) $-6 - 2 =$

(e) $3 - 7 =$ (f) $-7 + 3 =$ (g) $-1 - 5 =$ (h) $-3 + 3 =$

B5 Write a calculation which fits each of these moves on a number line.

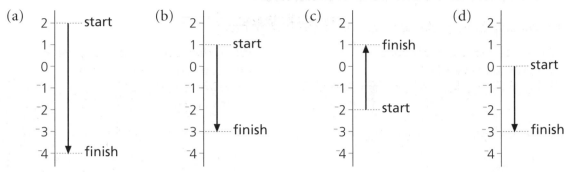

B6 Copy and complete these.

(a) $2 - ? = {}^-1$ (b) $2 - ? = {}^-2$ (c) $2 - ? = {}^-3$ (d) $? - 7 = {}^-5$

(e) $^-4 - ? = {}^-5$ (f) $? - 5 = 2$ (g) $? - 10 = {}^-2$ (h) $? - 4 = 4$

B7 Copy and complete these.

(a) $? + 3 = {}^-5$ (b) $? + 4 = 2$ (c) $4 + ? = 7$ (d) $4 - ? = {}^-7$

B8 Copy and complete these.

(a) $50 - 60 = ?$ (b) $^-30 - 50 = ?$ (c) $? - 60 = {}^-100$ (d) $^-90 + ? = {}^-10$

(e) $15 - ? = {}^-100$ (f) $100 - ? = {}^-21$ (g) $? - 18 = 42$ (h) $^-63 + ? = {}^-15$

B9 Work out the next three numbers in each of these.
For each one, write down how you found the next three numbers.

(a) 10, 8, 6, 4, ..., ..., ... (b) 7, 5, 3, 1, ..., ..., ...

(c) 40, 30, 20, 10, ..., ..., ... (d) $^-2, {}^-4, {}^-6, {}^-8$, ..., ..., ...

(e) Make up some questions of your own like this.
Give them to someone to see if they can work out the next three numbers.

B10 The temperature inside a house is 15°C.
The temperature outside is 20 degrees lower.

Which of these calculations do you do to work out the temperature outside?

| $^-20 - 15$ | | $15 - 20$ | | $^-15 - 20$ | | $^-15 + 20$ |

B11 Make three correct calculations by putting any of the numbers below into the spaces.

$$^-4 + ... = ...$$

| 6 | 5 | 3 | 2 | 1 | $^-1$ | $^-2$ | $^-3$ |

B12 Make three correct calculations by putting any of the numbers above into the spaces.

$$3 - ... = ...$$

C Adding negative numbers

Dana's class have a joke contest. The judges give points.

When they think a joke is good
they give scores like 5 or 7.

When they think a joke is awful
they can give negative scores.

The scores are added up.

What is the total score in each of these?

C1 What is the total score in each of these pictures?

(a)

(b)

(c)

(d)

C2 These are the scores for Ewan's joke.   These are the scores for Iain's joke.

| 1 | ⁻2 | ⁻3 | 5 |

| ⁻1 | ⁻3 | 3 | ⁻1 |

Who got the best total score?

C3 Work out the totals for these sets of scores.

(a) 1 ⁻2 ⁻2 1   (b) ⁻3 ⁻5 ⁻3 0   (c) 1 ⁻2 6 ⁻5

C4 Each of these sets of scores has a total of 2. Work out the missing scores.

(a) 3 ⁻1 ?   (b) ⁻2 ⁻3 1 ?   (c) 3 ⁻4 ⁻1 ⁻2 ?

C5 Do these additions.

(a) ⁻2 + ⁻1   (b) 2 + ⁻2 + 3   (c) ⁻1 + ⁻1 + ⁻2

(d) 4 + ⁻2 + ⁻5 + ⁻1   (e) ⁻6 + 9 + 1   (f) 5 + ⁻1 + ⁻3 + ⁻4

(g) ⁻3 + ⁻1 + 10   (h) 13 + ⁻2 + ⁻4   (i) ⁻10 + ⁻2 + 8 + 7

C6 The temperature at midday in a garden was recorded every day for a week in January.

5°C   ⁻1°C   5°C   3°C   ⁻2°C   5°C   6°C

What was the mean midday temperature for that week?

C7 The midnight temperatures were also recorded.

2°C   ⁻5°C   ⁻6°C   1°C   ⁻7°C   1°C   ⁻7°C

What was the mean midnight temperature?

C8 In a magic square each row, each column and each diagonal adds up to the same total (called the 'magic number').

Copy and complete these magic squares.

(a)

4		0
	1	
2	3	

(b)

1		⁻1
	2	
5	3	

(c)

⁻2	3	⁻4
⁻3		
		0

What progress have you made?

Statement	Evidence

I can do temperature calculations.

1 The temperature in my kitchen is 15°C. Work out the temperature in

(a) my fridge, 18 degrees colder than the kitchen

(b) my freezer, 32 degrees colder than the kitchen

2 At 6 a.m. the temperature was ⁻8°C. Work out the temperature at

(a) 9 a.m., when it was 4 degrees warmer than at 6 a.m.

(b) noon, 10 degrees warmer than at 6 a.m.

I can calculate with negative numbers.

3 Work these out.

(a) ⁻2 + 5 (b) ⁻10 + 8 (c) 4 − 8

(d) ⁻3 − 5 (e) ⁻3 + 3 (f) ⁻4 + 7

I can add negative numbers.

4 Work these out.

(a) 5 + ⁻3 (b) ⁻1 + ⁻4 (c) 4 + ⁻7

(d) 0 + ⁻2 (e) 1 + ⁻6 (f) ⁻3 + ⁻2

5 Work these out.

(a) 1 + ⁻5 + 2 (b) ⁻3 + ⁻4 + 4

(c) 3 + ⁻4 + ⁻1 (d) ⁻1 + ⁻2 + ⁻3

24 Ratio

This is about using ratios to describe mixtures and to compare quantities.
The work will help you

◆ solve simple ratio problems

◆ use the notation for ratio

A Recipes

Here is a recipe for light orange paint.

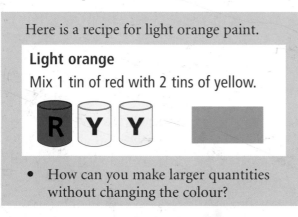

Light orange
Mix 1 tin of red with 2 tins of yellow.

● How can you make larger quantities
without changing the colour?

Here are some more shades of orange.

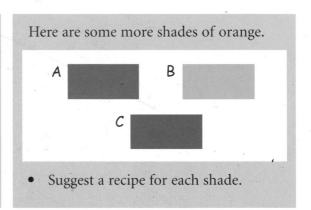

● Suggest a recipe for each shade.

A1 This is a recipe for light grey.

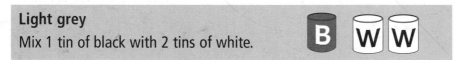

Light grey
Mix 1 tin of black with 2 tins of white.

(a) You want to make 3 times the amount in the recipe.
How many tins of white do you mix with 3 tins of black?

(b) How many tins of white do you mix with 6 tins of black?

A2 Here is a recipe for dark green.

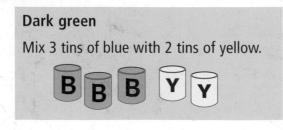

Dark green
Mix 3 tins of blue with 2 tins of yellow.

Copy and complete this mixing table.

	Blue	Yellow
2 times the recipe	6 tins	
3 times the recipe		
5 times the recipe		
10 times the recipe		

A3 This is the recipe for light pink.

Light pink
Mix 1 litre of red with 4 litres of white.

(a) How many litres of white do you mix with 3 litres of red?

(b) (i) How many litres of white do you mix with 2 litres of red?

　　(ii) How much light pink paint would this give you altogether?

(c) How many litres of **red** do you mix with 20 litres of white?

A4

Lemonade
Mix 1 part lemon juice with 4 parts fizzy water.

(a) You have 2 litres of lemon juice.
How much fizzy water do you mix with it?

(b) (i) How much fizzy water do you mix with 5 litres of lemon juice?

　　(ii) How much lemonade would this give you?

A5 Here is a recipe for making light green paint.

Light green
2 parts blue to 5 parts yellow

Copy the table on the right and fill it in.

Litres of blue	Litres of yellow	Litres of light green
4		
6		
8		
10		

A6 This is a recipe for Spinach Sauté.

(a) Rui wants to make Spinach Sauté for 6 people.
How many onions would she need?

(b) What weight of unsalted peanuts would
she need to make this for 6 people?

(c) What weight of fresh spinach would
she need to make this for 6 people?

(d) Write out a recipe for Spinach Sauté to serve 6 people.

A7 Write out a recipe for Spinach Sauté to serve 4 people.

A8 David wants to make Spinach Sauté for one person.

(a) What weight of spinach should he use?

(b) What weight of margarine should he use?

Spinach Sauté
(Serves 2)
500 g fresh spinach
150 g unsalted peanuts
1 large onion
150 g margarine

A9 This is a recipe for Kedgeree.

(a) How many eggs would you need to make Kedgeree for 12 people?

(b) What weight of kipper fillets would you need to make Kedgeree for 8 people?

(c) How much cooked rice would you need to make Kedgeree for one person?

(d) How much cooked rice would you need to make Kedgeree for three people?

Kedgeree
(Serves 4)

500 g cooked rice

250 g kipper fillets

4 hard-boiled eggs

150 g butter

8 tbsps. single cream

B Ratios

This block is made with 2 red cubes and 1 yellow cube.

This is a pile of blocks like the one above.

Whatever the size of the pile, there will always be **2 red cubes to every 1 yellow cube**.

We say the **ratio** of reds to yellows is **2 to 1**.

We can also say that the ratio of yellows to reds is 1 to 2.

**ratio of reds to yellows
2 to 1**

B1 What is the ratio of red cubes to yellow cubes in each of these?

(a)

(b)

(c)

(d)

138

B2 This box contains 6 red beads and 12 yellow beads.

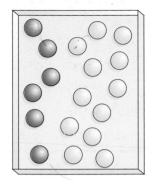

(a) Can you make the beads into designs like this with none left over?

(b) Can you make the beads into designs like this with none left over?

(c) What is the ratio of **reds** to **yellows** in the box?

(d) What is the ratio of **yellows** to **reds** in the box?

B3 Here are six sets of beads.

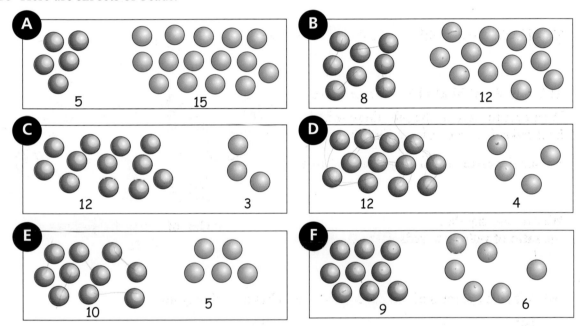

(a) Which set can be made into designs like this with no beads left over? Write down the ratio of reds to blues for this set.

(b) Which set can be made into designs like this with no beads left over? Write down the ratio of reds to blues for this set.

C Using shorthand

The ratio 1 to 3 can be written as 1 : 3.

The order is important.
So for these beads we can write
  ratio of green to yellow = 1 : 3.

For these beads
  ratio of green to yellow = 3 : 1.

C1 Write down, using shorthand notation, the ratio of red to yellow beads in each of these.

(a)

(b)

(c)

C2 Write the ratio of blue to yellow paint using shorthand notation.

(a)

(b)

(c)

(d)

C3 Write these as ratios using shorthand notation.

(a) 1 litre of lime juice is mixed with 4 litres of water.

(b) Three buckets of sand are mixed with one bucket of cement.

(c) 3 cups of sugar are mixed with 2 cups of flour.

C4 To make mint tea you can mix two teaspoons of green tea with one of dried mint. Copy and complete this statement.

The ratio of green tea to dried mint =

What progress have you made?

Statement

I can work out quantities from a recipe for a mixture.

Evidence

1 Orange fizz is made by mixing 1 part of orange juice with 5 parts of lemonade.

(a) How much lemonade do you mix with 3 litres of orange juice?

(b) How much orange juice do you need to mix with 25 litres of lemonade?

Statement

I can write ratios using shorthand.

Evidence

2 Write the ratio of full to empty glasses.

(a)

(b)

Review 4

1 Work out the angles labelled with letters in these diagrams.

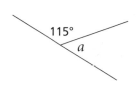

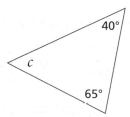

2

Use the numbers above to copy and complete these statements.

(a) ... is a prime number.   (b) ... is a multiple of 12.   (c) ... is a factor of 45.

(d) ... is the square root of ...   (e) ... has 5 as a factor.

3 Write TRUE or FALSE for each of these statements.
   If the statement is false, give an example that shows why it is false.

(a) A number which has both 2 and 3 as factors must also have 6 as a factor.

(b) A shape with rotation symmetry also has reflection symmetry.

(c) If you are told three lengths you can always make a triangle
     whose sides are these three lengths.

4 The list shows the times of some TV
   programmes on a new channel.

1900	Westenders
1930	Pet Savers
2015	News and weather
2030	Film: You only live once
2215	Time for Answers
2255	Little Sister
2340	Closedown

(a) Natalie arrives home at 6:25 p.m.
     How long is it till Westenders starts?

(b) How long is the film on for?

(c) How long is Little Sister on for?

(d) Michael watches TV from the start of
     Pet Savers until the end of Time for Answers.
     How long does he watch TV for?

5 Copy and complete these.

(a) $^-3 + 7 = ?$ (b) $^-8 + 5 = ?$ (c) $^-3 + ? = 2$ (d) $^-7 + ? = ^-3$

(e) $^-3 - ? = ^-10$ (f) $3 - ? = ^-2$ (g) $2 + ^-7 = ?$ (h) $8 + ^-5 = ?$

(i) $7 + ? = 4$ (j) $5 + ? = ^-2$ (k) $7 + ^-2 + 5 = ?$ (l) $^-6 + 10 + ^-2 = ?$

6 An egg box contains 12 eggs of which 4 are rotten.
   An egg is chosen at random from the box.
   What is the probability of choosing a rotten egg?

7 Look at this family of cats.

Describe each of these translations accurately.

(a) Cat C to cat B

(b) Cat A to cat B

(c) Cat D to cat A

(d) Cat B to cat D

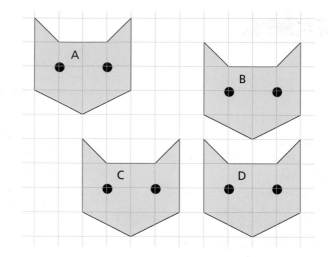

8 This is a recipe for Vegan Cheesecake.

(a) How many tablespoons (tbs) of lemon juice would you need to make 18 slices of Vegan Cheesecake?

(b) How much tofu would you need to make 12 slices of Vegan Cheesecake?

(c) How much margarine would you need to make 24 slices?

(d) How much soya milk would you need to make 3 slices?

> ### Vegan Cheesecake
> **(Makes 6 slices)**
>
> 500 g tofu
> 200 ml soya milk
> 300 g crushed digestive biscuits
> 100 g margarine
> 1 tbs of lemon juice
> Half a jar of strawberry jam

9 Work these out, writing each answer in its simplest form.

(a) $\frac{3}{13} + \frac{5}{13}$ (b) $\frac{1}{8} + \frac{3}{8}$ (c) $\frac{7}{9} - \frac{5}{9}$ (d) $\frac{11}{12} - \frac{7}{12}$

10 Write these as ratios using shorthand notation.

(a) 1 cup of oats is mixed with 3 cups of water.

(b) Three pots of compost are mixed with two pots of sand.

(c) Use 3 red geraniums to each white one.

11 Sobia is making some chokers from beads.
Here are some of her designs.

   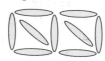   

Pattern 1   Pattern 2   Pattern 3

(a) How many beads does Sobia need for pattern 4?

(b) How many beads does Sobia need for pattern 10?

(c) Write out a rule using letters that says how many beads (*b*) you need for each pattern number (*p*).

142

Index

acute angle 113–114
addition
    of decimals 7–8, 11
    of fractions 34–35
    of negative whole numbers 130–134
algebraic expression
    for nth pattern in a sequence 19–27
    simplifying 57–60, 99–104
angles
    estimating and measuring 113–114
    of a triangle 118
    on a straight line 113–115
    round a point 116–117
    types 113–114
area of rectangle and triangle 91–93

calendar 124
clock, 12-hour and 24-hour 125–127
collecting like terms 57–60, 99–104
congruent triangles and quadrilaterals 10

dates 124
decimals 7–9, 11–17
division
    of decimals 14–17, 81–82
    of whole numbers 75–81

expression
    for nth pattern in a sequence 19–27
    simplifying 57–60, 99–104

factor 5, 95–96
formula for linear sequence from patterns 19–27
fractions
    adding and subtracting 34–35
    equivalence 32–34, 42–43
    for probabilities 40–43
    from pie chart 62–63
    identifying 6, 29–30
    of quantity 6, 30–31

general statement, disproof by a counter-example 123
graph of linear function 25–27

linear sequence from set of geometrical patterns 19–27

money 11–17, 45–46, 47, 83
multiple 4–5, 94–95
multiplication
    of decimals 7–8, 11–13
    of whole numbers 4–5

negative whole numbers, addition 130–134

obtuse angle 113–114

percentage
    from pie chart 64–66
    of a quantity in simple cases 48–53
pie chart 62–66
prime number 5, 96–97
probability
    estimating from results of experiment 67–72
    from known proportions 38–43

ratio 136–140
reflection 84–85
reflex angle 113–114
rotation 86–87
rounding to nearest penny 13

simplifying algebraic expression 57–60, 99–104
square number 5, 97–98
square root 97–98
subtraction
    of decimals 8–9
    of fractions 34

time 125–129
timetable 128–129
transformations of points and shapes 84–89
translation 88
triangle, accurate construction 119–121
two-way table 106–110

unit cost 13–17, 45–46